高等院校物流管理专业系列教材·物流企业岗位培训系列教材

PRACTICAL ENGLISH COURSE
OF FREIGHT FORWARDING

货运代理英语

陈永生　鄢　莉◎主　编
帅　京　邹　蓉◎副主编

清華大学出版社
北京

内 容 简 介

本书根据国际物流货运代理发展的新特点,按照货运代理的业务流程和操作规范,系统介绍询价议价、接单揽货、仓储订舱、包装、装货、调拨转运、卸货、制单、报关报检、结算、索赔与理赔等货运代理英语基础知识,并通过实训提高应用能力。

本书具有知识系统、案例丰富、实用性强等特点,既可作为普通高等院校本科物流管理、工商管理等专业的首选教材,同时兼顾高职高专、应用型大学的教学,也可用于物流企业员工在职培训,并为外贸、物流企业开拓国际业务提供有益的指导。

本书封面贴有清华大学出版社防伪标签,无标签者不得销售。

版权所有,侵权必究。举报:010-62782989,beiqinquan@tup.tsinghua.edu.cn。

图书在版编目(CIP)数据

货运代理英语 / 陈永生,鄢莉主编. -- 北京:清华大学出版社,2025.2.
(高等院校物流管理专业系列教材). -- ISBN 978-7-302-68312-4

Ⅰ. F511.41

中国国家版本馆 CIP 数据核字第 20254WY355 号

责任编辑:贺　岩
封面设计:汉风唐韵
责任校对:王荣静
责任印制:刘海龙

出版发行:清华大学出版社
网　　址:https://www.tup.com.cn,https://www.wqxuetang.com
地　　址:北京清华大学学研大厦A座　　邮　编:100084
社 总 机:010-83470000　　邮　购:010-62786544
投稿与读者服务:010-62776969,c-service@tup.tsinghua.edu.cn
质量反馈:010-62772015,zhiliang@tup.tsinghua.edu.cn

印 装 者:三河市东方印刷有限公司
经　　销:全国新华书店
开　　本:185mm×230mm　　印　张:14.5　　字　数:246千字
版　　次:2025年2月第1版　　印　次:2025年2月第1次印刷
定　　价:49.00元

产品编号:099461-01

高等院校物流管理专业系列教材·物流企业岗位培训系列教材

编审委员会

主　任

　　牟惟仲　中国物流技术协会理事长、教授级高级工程师

副主任

　　翁心刚　北京物资学院副院长、教授
　　冀俊杰　中国物资信息中心原副主任、总工程师
　　张昌连　中国商业信息中心原主任、总工程师
　　吴　明　中国物流技术协会副理事长兼秘书长、高级工程师
　　李大军　中国物流技术协会副秘书长、中国计算机协会理事

委　员

　　张建国　王海文　刘　华　孙　旭　刘徐方　赵立群
　　孙　军　田振中　李耀华　李爱华　郑强国　刘子玉
　　林玲玲　王　艳　刘丽艳　袁　峰　卢亚丽　周　伟
　　张劲珊　董　铁　罗佩华　吴青梅　于汶艳　郑秀恋
　　刘芳娜　刘慧敏　赵　迪　刘阳威　李秀华　罗松涛

总　编

　　李大军

副总编

　　王海文　刘徐方　刘　华　田振中　郑强国

序言

物流是国民经济的重要组成部分，也是我国经济发展新的增长点。2020年10月，党的十九届五中全会审议通过《中共中央关于制定国民经济和社会发展第十四个五年规划和二〇三五年远景目标的建议》，为我国物流产业发展指明了前进方向，并对进一步加快我国现代物流发展、提高经济运行质量与效益、实现可持续发展战略、推进我国经济体制与经济增长方式的根本性转变，具有非常重要而深远的意义。

"一带一路"建设和我国与沿线国家互联互通的快速推进，以及全球电子商务的迅猛发展，不仅有力地促进了我国物流产业的国际化发展，而且使我国迅速融入全球经济一体化的进程，中国市场国际化的特征越发凸显。

物流不但涉及交通运输、仓储配送、通关报检等业务环节，同时也涉及国际贸易、国际商务活动等外向型经济领域。当前面对世界经济的迅猛发展和国际市场激烈竞争的压力，如何加强物流科技知识的推广应用、加快物流专业技能型应用人才的培养，已成为我国经济转型发展过程中亟待解决的问题。

针对我国高等职业教育院校物流教材陈旧和知识老化的问题，为了满足国家经济发展和就业需要，满足物流行业规模发展对操作技能型人才的需求，在中国物流技术协会的支持下，我们组织北京物资学院、大连工业大学、北京城市学院、吉林工程技术师范学院、北京财贸职业学院、郑州大学、哈尔滨理工大学、燕山大学、浙江工业大学、河北理工大学、华北水利水电大学、江西财经大学、山东外贸职业学院、吉林财经大学、广东理工大学等全国20多个省市应用型大学及高职高专院校物流管理专业的主讲教师和物流企业经理共同编写了此套教材，旨在提高高等院校物流管理专业学生和物流行业从业者的专业技术素质，更好地服务于我国物流产业和物流经济。

作为普通高等院校物流管理专业的特色教材，本套教材融入了物流运营管理的最新教学理念，注重与时俱进，根据物流业发展的新形势和新特点，依照物流活动的基本过程和规律，全面贯彻国家"十四五"教育发展规划，按照物流企业对人才的需求模式，加强实践能力训练，注重校企结合、贴近物流企业业务实际，注重新设施设备操作技术的掌握，强化实践技能与岗位应用能力培训，并注重教学内容和教材结构的创新。

　　本套教材根据高等院校物流管理专业教学大纲和课程设置，对帮助学生尽快熟悉物流操作规程与业务管理，毕业后顺利走上社会具有特殊意义，因而既可作为本科或高职院校物流管理专业的教材，也可作为物流、商务贸易等企业在职员工的培训用书。

中国物流技术协会理事长　牟惟仲
2022 年 10 月于北京

前言

当前,随着国家"一带一路、互联互通"总体发展策略的制定和实施,随着我国大批企业跨出国门、参与全球经济活动,面对物流市场国际化的迅速发展与激烈竞争,对从事国际物流货运代理人员的素质要求越来越高,社会物资流通和物流产业发展急需大量具有知识技能、懂操作、会应用的复合实用型货运代理英语专门人才。

外语是涉外服务的工具,也是对外交流的重要手段。英语是国际经济业务的通用语言和主要交际工具,国际物流货运代理从业人员的英语应用水平直接影响着我国物流业的发展速度与服务质量。为了满足日益增长的外向型物流市场需求,培养社会急需的国际物流货运代理运作应用型外语人才,我们组织全国多所高等院校中长年从事货运代理英语教学和实践活动的专家教授共同精心编写了本书,旨在提高大学生和物流企业从业者的专业英语应用水平,更好地服务于我国的物流产业。

货运代理英语是大学物流管理专业的核心课程,也是国际物流货运代理从业者必须掌握的关键技能。本书作为普通高等教育物流管理专业的特色教材,全书共 12 章,以学生应用能力培养为主线,坚持科学发展观,严格按照教育部"加强职业教育、突出实践技能培养"的要求,根据国际物流货运代理发展的新特点,按照货运代理业务流程和操作规范,系统介绍询价议价、接单揽货、仓储订舱、包装、装货、调拨转运、卸货、制单、报关报检、结算、索赔与理赔等货运代理英语基础知识,并通过指导学生实训,提高其应用能力。

本书融入了国际物流货运代理英语最新的实践教学理念,突出"以任务为导向,以学生为核心"的教育模式,注重从业就业能力实训,因此既可作为普通高等院校本科物流管理、工商管理、国际贸易等专业的首选教材,同时兼顾高职高专、应用型大学的教学,也可用于物流企业员工在职岗位培训，并为外贸、物流企业开拓国际业务提供有益的学习指导。

　　本书由李大军筹划并具体组织；陈永生和鄢莉为主编，帅京、邹蓉为副主编；全书由陈永生统稿，由刘徐方审定。编写分工：牟惟仲（序言），鄢莉（第1章、第7章、第10章），陈永生（第2章、第5章、第6章、第9章），帅京（第3章、第4章、第11章），邹蓉（第8章、第12章）；李晓新（文字修改、教学课件制作）。

　　在本书编写过程中，我们参阅了国内外国际物流货运代理英语最新的书刊资料和各国颁布实施的相关法律法规，并得到业界有关专家学者的具体指导，在此一并致谢。

　　为了配合教学，我们特为本书配备了电子课件，任课教师可以扫描书后二维码免费下载使用。因编者水平有限，书中难免有疏漏和不足，恳请同行和读者批评指正。

编　者
2024年8月

目录

Unit 1　Enquiry and Bargaining ······················· 1

　　Section 1　Theme Lead-in ······················· 2
　　Section 2　Conversations and Warm-up ······················· 4
　　Section 3　Format Writings and Practical Usages ······················· 7
　　Section 4　Skills Training and Case Study Samples ······················· 13
　　Section 5　Elevating Vision and Useful Expressions ······················· 16

Unit 2　Canvassion ······················· 18

　　Section 1　Theme Lead-in ······················· 19
　　Section 2　Conversations and Warm-up ······················· 20
　　Section 3　Format Writings and Practical Usages ······················· 23
　　Section 4　Skills Training and Case Study Samples ······················· 27
　　Section 5　Elevating Vision and Useful Expressions ······················· 30

Unit 3　Warehousing and Chartering Space ······················· 33

　　Section 1　Theme Lead-in ······················· 34
　　Section 2　Conversations and Warm-up ······················· 36
　　Section 3　Format Writings and Practical Usages ······················· 39
　　Section 4　Skills Training and Case Study Samples ······················· 43
　　Section 5　Elevating Vision and Useful Expressions ······················· 47

Unit 4　Packaging ······················· 49

　　Section 1　Theme Lead-in ······················· 50
　　Section 2　Conversations and Warm-up ······················· 53

Section 3	Format Writings and Practical Usages	56
Section 4	Skills Training and Case Study Samples	61
Section 5	Elevating Vision and Useful Expressions	64

Unit 5　Loading　68

Section 1	Theme Lead-in	69
Section 2	Conversations and Warm-up	72
Section 3	Format Writings and Practical Usages	74
Section 4	Skills Training and Case Study Samples	79
Section 5	Elevating Vision and Useful Expressions	83

Unit 6　Allocation and Transshipment　85

Section 1	Theme Lead-in	86
Section 2	Conversations and Warm-up	87
Section 3	Format Writings and Practical Usages	91
Section 4	Skills Training and Case Study Samples	97
Section 5	Elevating Vision and Useful Expressions	100

Unit 7　Unloading　103

Section 1	Theme Lead-in	104
Section 2	Conversations and Warm-up	108
Section 3	Format Writings and Practical Usages	110
Section 4	Skills Training and Case Study Samples	114
Section 5	Elevating Vision and Useful Expressions	117

Unit 8　Documentation　120

Section 1	Theme Lead-in	121
Section 2	Conversations and Warm-up	123
Section 3	Format Writings and Practical Usages	126
Section 4	Skills Training and Case Study Samples	136
Section 5	Elevating Vision and Useful Expressions	140

Unit 9　Commodity Inspection　142

Section 1	Theme Lead-in	143

	Section 2	Conversations and Warm-up	146
	Section 3	Format Writings and Practical Usages	149
	Section 4	Skills Training and Case Study Samples	152
	Section 5	Elevating Vision and Useful Expressions	156

Unit 10　Customs Clearance ………………………………………… 158

	Section 1	Theme Lead-in	159
	Section 2	Conversations and Warm-up	162
	Section 3	Format Writings and Practical Usages	165
	Section 4	Skills Training and Case Study Samples	175
	Section 5	Elevating Vision and Useful Expressions	178

Unit 11　Account Settlement ………………………………………… 181

	Section 1	Theme Lead-in	182
	Section 2	Conversations and Warm-up	185
	Section 3	Format Writings and Practical Usages	188
	Section 4	Skills Training and Case Study Samples	191
	Section 5	Elevating Vision and Useful Expressions	195

Unit 12　Claim and Settlement ………………………………………… 198

	Section 1	Theme Lead-in	199
	Section 2	Conversations and Warm-up	202
	Section 3	Format Writings and Practical Usages	205
	Section 4	Skills Training and Case Study Samples	209
	Section 5	Elevating Vision and Useful Expressions	213

References ………………………………………………………………… 216

Unit 1

Enquiry and Bargaining

Learning Objectives

- To know the main elements in the quotation for freight services
- To know the basic rules for a valid offer and an acceptance
- To learn the expressions in making enquiries and quotations

Skill Developing Objectives

- To develop communication skills in the enquiry and quotation for freight services
- To develop writing skills in the enquiry and quotation for freight services

Section 1 Theme Lead-in

Read the following passage to get a better understanding of this unit.

Quotation after Enquiry

First of all, European inquiring parties expect a firm quotation within three days. If you cannot, for some reasons, react within these three days, make sure someone in your organization gives a message: asking for further details, explaining or excusing the delay, and mentioning the period in which a firm reaction can be expected, plus the reason for it, and asking whether that is acceptable.

You need to know more about the customer before you make your offer. A useful source of information is certainly the company's website and more details can be found through trade directories as well.

Make sure you have all the tools available on your own end, including a good brochure, a dynamic website and instruments to show your professionalism contained in a company profile.

Last but not least, train and instruct your assistants with precision to communicate properly when the customer contacts you via the phone. Your employee who is responsible for commercial issues should make a basic instruction manual for your assistants.

In order to make a good quotation which includes all the necessary information, you should follow certain steps:

Your quotation should bear an identification reference number as well and be clearly traceable from the customer's end. Moreover, your own employees must be fully aware of this identification number and recognize it immediately. The reason for this is simply that it shows the interest in the customer.

Confirm the quantities which were requested and make clear that your prices are based on these volumes.

Prices should be preferably in the currency which was requested but make clear which prices belong to which quantities. Although you may be at risk, in this phase it is more important to accommodate to your customer's wishes than to secure all the risks. Prior investigation of the credibility of the customer may reduce the possible threats.

Provide a realistic delivery time schedule but have it checked with your production manager first. This can certainly prevent any obstructions once the order comes through.

Limit the acceptance time of your offer to be able to review the prices and delivery schedule when that time has lapsed. Mention the acceptance validity of the offer and make clear that you have to review your quotation after that date.

Notes

1. First of all, European inquiring parties expect a firm quotation within three days.
   首先,欧洲的询价方期待能在三日内收到对方报的实价。

2. Asking for further details, explaining or excusing the delay, and mentioning the period in which a firm reaction can be expected, plus the reason for it, and asking whether that is acceptable.
   进一步询问信息,为延迟报价做出解释或道歉,提出报实价所需的时间并解释原因,并询问对方是否可以接受。

3. You need to know more about the customer before you make your offer.
   在报盘之前,你需要对顾客有更多的了解。

4. Make sure you have all the tools available on your own end, including a good brochure, a dynamic website and instruments to show your professionalism contained in a company profile.
   确保你拥有所需的一切工具,包括产品手册、动态网站,以及公司简介中体现专业性的各种设备。

5. Last but not least, train and instruct your assistants with precision to communicate properly when the customer contacts you via the phone.
   最后但同样重要的是,一定要指导你的助理在接听客户来电时恰当沟通。

6. Your quotation should bear an identification reference number and be clearly traceable from the customer's end.
   你的报价需要包含用于识别的参考码,并确保客户可以追踪到。

7. Confirm the quantities which were requested and make clear that your prices are based on these volumes.
   确认需求数量并且声明报价基于这些数量。

8. Prices should be preferably in the currency which was requested but make clear which prices belong to which quantities.
   价格应以所要求的货币为准,但应使价格与数量一一对应。

9. Although you may be at risk, in this phase it is more important to accommodate

to your customer's wishes than to secure all the risks.

虽然你可能有点冒险,但在这一阶段迎合客户的意愿比规避风险更加重要。

10. Prior investigation of the credibility of the customer may reduce the possible threats.

    提前对客户进行信誉度调查可以减少风险。

11. Limit the acceptance time of your offer to be able to review the prices and delivery schedule when that time has lapsed.

    规定报价的期限,以便在这一报价到期时重新定价和安排交货。

12. Mention the acceptance validity of the offer and make clear that you have to review your quotation after that date.

    提及报价的有效期,并声明超过这一日期后你将重新报价。

 Problems Solving

1. Discuss with your partners about the procedure in forming a contract.
2. Match the following sentences with the proper terms in the box.

   | acceptance   firm offer   non-firm offer   counter offer   enquiry |

   (1) The offer is subject to our final confirmation.   (   )
   (2) The offer is valid subject to your reply reaching us by the end of May. (   )
   (3) Could you offer us your lowest price for freight forwarding services?   (   )
   (4) Your price is not competitive. Could you reduce the price to $70?   (   )
   (5) We accept your offer of $0.67/piece and please find attached our request for sample.   (   )

 # Section 2　Conversations and Warm-up

 Conversation 1　Bargaining over Freight Rate

(*B is Ms. Li, the clerk of Hengtong Company, who is talking with A, William Smith, a potential client.*)

A: I'm interested in all kinds of your products, but this time I would like to order some fireworks and mosquito coil incense. Please quote us C.I.F. Rangoon.

B: Please let us know the quantity required so that we can work out the premium and freight charges.

A: I'm going to place a trial order for 1,000 units of a dozen fireworks and 500 cartons of mosquito coil incense.

B: All right. Here are our F.O.B. price lists. All the prices are subject to our final confirmation.

A: Your price is reasonable but I wonder if you would give us a discount. You know for the products like yours we usually get a 2% or 3% discount from European suppliers.

B: We usually offer on a net basis only. Many of our clients have been doing very well on this quoted price.

A: Discounts will more or less encourage us to make every effort to push sales of your products.

B: The quantity you ordered is much smaller than those of others. If you can manage to boost it a bit, we'll consider giving you a better discount.

A: As far as a trial order is concerned, the quantity is by no means small. And generally speaking, we like to profit from a trial order. I hope you'll be able to meet our requirements.

B: Well, as this is the first deal between us, we agree to give you a 1% discount as a special encouragement.

A: 1%? That's too low of a rate. Could you see your way to increase it to 2%?

B: I'm afraid we have really made a great concession, and could not go any further.

A: Well. I don't think it's wise for us to insist on our own price. I suggest we meet each other halfway. It seems this is the only proposal for me to accept. I'll come again tomorrow to discuss it in detail.

B: All right. See you tomorrow.

Conversation 2　Enquiry and Quotation

(*A is William Smith, an exporter from DLA Clothing Company, who is talking with B, Wang Yong, a sales manager of a logistics company.*)

A: Good morning, Mr. Wang.

B: Good morning, Mr. Smith. Thanks for your enquiry of August 20.

A: You know we are very interested in your quotation. Could you show me your latest freight service catalogues?

B: Sure, here you are.

A: Thanks. Is it your best price?

B: Yes, it is. And for the quantities of more than 100 MTs, we can offer a discount of 15% on our price list.

A: That's great! Please let me know the shipping schedules in recent months.

B: OK. I'll send you the details as soon as I get them.

A: Very good. We'll be expecting to hear from you.

 Conversation 3　Request for Quotation and Payment Terms

(*A is Miss Lin, a receptionist of a logistics company, who is welcoming B, Jason, a businessman from an export company.*)

A: Good morning. Welcome to our company. What can I do for you?

B: Good morning. I learned from the newspaper that your company can transport large machinery and equipment, right?

A: Yes, we can. What kind of machines do you want to transport?

B: We have some urban cleaning machinery to be exported to the United States. Would you please give me the quotation with details of your freight prices?

A: Sure. This is our catalogue. Please have a look.

B: How should we pay for your services?

A: We usually accept the payment by cheque when the whole delivery process is over.

B: Okay. Is there any time limit for making the payment?

A: You are required to make the payment within five days after you receive our bill. For the overdue account, we charge 0.5% of the total arrearage per day.

B: I see. Thanks for the information.

 Warm-up

A. Match the definitions in Column B with the terms in Column A.

A	B
1. FOB(Free on Board)	A. an irrevocable offer made by a merchant
2. ceiling price	B. a trade term requiring the seller to deliver goods on board a vessel designated by the buyer
3. CIF(Cost, Insurance and Freight)	C. a government-imposed price control or limit on how high a price is charged for a product

A	B
4. firm offer	D. a trade term requiring the seller to arrange for the carriage of goods by sea to a port of destination, and provide the buyer with the documents necessary to obtain the goods from the carrier
5. DAT (Delivered at Terminal)	E. an international commercial term whereby the seller pays all transport costs

B. The following is a passage about offer and quotation. Fill in the blanks with the words given in the box and then discuss with your partners about the differences between a quotation and an offer.

negotiation   conclude   customer   role   conditions

Offer is an expression in which its offeror is willing to (1)_____ a transaction with an offeree on terms and (2)_____ mentioned, it is a reply to an enquiry from a (3)_____. In international trade practice, quotation, which is the reply to the inquiry's requests, can also play the (4)_____ of the offer. It is often made by letter, fax or E-mail. It is the first step in business (5)_____.

C. Make up a dialogue according to the following situation.

Student A works as a sales manager in a logistics company, and Student B is an exporter who is willing to know the quotation for freight services. Student A and Student B will act out a dialogue about the quotation for freight services.

The dialogue should cover the following information: greeting, the information of the goods to be delivered, the quotation and payment terms for freight services.

Section 3 Format Writings and Practical Usages

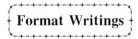

Read the following passage, and answer the questions.

Offer and Acceptance

Offer and acceptance are elements required for the formation of a legally binding contract.

An offer is an expression of willingness to contract on certain terms, made with the intention that it shall become binding as soon as it is accepted by the offeree. The expression of an offer may take different forms, such as a letter, advertisement, fax, email and even conduct, as long as it communicates the basis on which the offeror is prepared to contract.

A valid offer usually includes at least the following four terms: delivery date, price, terms of payment and detailed description of the item on offer including a fair description of the condition or type of service. An invitation to treat is not an offer, but an indication of a person's willingness to negotiate a contract.

An acceptance is a promise or act on the part of an offeree indicating a willingness to be bound by the terms and conditions contained in an offer. There are several rules dealing with the communication of acceptance:

- The acceptance must be communicated, the offeror cannot include an Acceptance by Silence clause.
- An offer can only be accepted by the offeree, that is, the person to whom the offer is made.
- The offeree should not materially alter the terms of the offer.

 Problems Solving

1. What elements are required for the formation of a legally binding contract?
2. According to the passage, what terms are usually included in a valid offer?
3. Could you give an example of an invitation to treat?
4. Can a person to whom the offer is not made accept the offer? Why?
5. If an offeree alters the term of payment in an offer, is his acceptance valid? Why?

 Writing Samples

Letter 1 Enquiry

August 15, 2024

Dear Sir,

We have learned from the website that your company can transport large machinery.

We run crane retail business and we are interested in the machines in Canada. Would you please quote us your rate for the shipment from Shanghai to Port of Montreal and send us details of your sailing and the time usually taken for the voyage?

It will be of great help if you could supply the best shipping line between Canada and China.

Yours faithfully,

Letter 2　Quotation

August 16, 2024

Dear Sir or Madame,

　　Thank you for your Enquiry of 15 August. We are pleased to hear that you are interested in our freight services.

　　We would like to offer you the best price from Shanghai to Port of Montreal. Our quotation is as follows:

　　1. BRING UP GOODS FEE　　　　　USD 90.00
　　2. CUSTOMS CLEARANCE　　　　　USD 200.00
　　3. BEAT SINGLE FEE　　　　　　　USD 38.00
　　4. DEST LOCAL CHARGE　　　　　USD 110.00
　　5. DOCUMENT FEE　　　　　　　　USD 60.00
　　6. LOAD & UNLOAD CHARGE　　　USD 100.00
　　7. RECEIVE 2% AGENT SERVICE CHARGE OF INVOICE GOODS VALUE

　　Enclosed please find different containers' descriptions and shipping schedules in recent months.

　　We must stress that this offer can remain open for three days only and we look forward to receiving an order from you.

Yours faithfully,

Letter 3　Counter Offer

August 21, 2024

Dear Sir or Madame,

　　Thank you very much for your prompt reply and detailed quotation.

　　We regret to say that your offer is not in the least encouraging. There is a big difference between your price and those of your competitors. We wish you will reconsider your price and give us a new offer, so that there can be a possibility for us to meet halfway.

We are expecting your early reply.

Yours faithfully,

Practical Usages

1. Enquiry 询价

1) To state the source of information and the intention to cooperate
说明从何处获知公司信息,表明合作意愿
- We have learned from the newspaper that your company can transport large machinery.
我方从报纸上得知贵公司从事大型机械运输业务。
- We have seen your forwarder ad in the newspaper and we are interested in your freight services.
从报纸上看到贵公司的货运代理广告,我们对此很感兴趣。

2) To state the expectation for freight service catalogues or a price list
索要货运服务目录或报价单
- Would you please quote us your rate for the shipment from Shanghai to Port of Montreal and send us details of your sailing and the time usually taken for the voyage?
请问可否报上海至蒙特利尔港货运价,并告知我方该航线及航程的详细情况?
- Please send your current/latest catalogue/price list/brochure.
请寄送贵方最新产品目录/价目表/产品手册。
- Please quote your best/most competitive/lowest freight price.
请报最优惠/最具竞争力/最低货运价格。

3) To state the expectation for future cooperation
对未来合作的期待
- If your freight service prices are competitive, we shall cooperate with you on a regular basis.
如果贵方货运价格具有竞争力,我们将长期和贵公司合作。
- If you can let us have a competitive quotation, we trust business will result.
如果贵方报价具有竞争力,相信我们将展开合作。

2. Quotation 报价

1) To express the appreciation for receiving the enquiry
   对询价的感谢
   - Thank you for your Enquiry of 15 August. We are pleased to hear that you are interested in our freight services.
     感谢贵方 8 月 15 日的询价，很高兴贵方对我们的货代服务感兴趣。
   - We are very pleased to have received your Enquiry dated Sept. 18.
     很荣幸收到贵方 9 月 18 日的询价。

2) To reply to the enquiry in detail
   详细回复询价信息
   - We would like to offer you the best price from Shanghai to Port of Montreal.
     现向贵方报上海至蒙特利尔港最低价。
   - Enclosed please find different containers' descriptions and shipping schedules in recent months.
     现附寄不同规格集装箱说明及近几个月船运安排，请查收。
   - We arrange shipments to any part of the world, we are sending you our latest freight service catalogues.
     我们承揽发往世界各地的货运业务，现寄送最新货运服务目录。

3) Stating the validity of quotation
   表明报价的有效期
   - We must stress that this offer can remain open for three days only.
     我们必须强调此报价只在三日内有效。
   - The offer is subject to our confirmation.
     以我方确认为准。
   - We cannot consider these prices firm for an indefinite period because of the situation on the present market.
     鉴于目前市场的行情，我们无法长期保持这一价格不变。

4) To state the expectation for the order or cooperation
   对订单或合作的期待
   - We look forward to receiving an order from you.
     期待您的订单。
   - We feel confident that you will find the services both excellent in quality and reasonable in price.
     相信贵方会觉得我方服务上乘、价格合理。

3. Counter Offer 还盘

1) Thanks for the quotation
对对方报价表示感谢
- Thank you for your prompt reply and detailed quotation.
  感谢您的及时回复和详细报价。
- We thank you for the letter of August 15, covering the latest quotation for your freight services.
  感谢贵方8月15日来信,从信中我们获知了贵方货运最新报价。

2) To decline the quotation and giving the reasons
谢绝报价并说明原因
- We regret to say that your offer is not in the least encouraging. There is a big difference between your price and those of your competitors.
  我们很遗憾您的报价太高,与同类竞争者的价格差距过大。
- We find your freight prices are too high to be acceptable.
  我们认为贵方货运价格太高、无法接受。
- Your quoted price is out of line with the prevailing level.
  您的报价与同行业价格水平不符。

3) Expectation of reply
期待回复
- We wish you will reconsider your price and give us a new offer, so that there can be a possibility for us to meet halfway.
  我们希望您能重新考虑,给出新的报价,以便我们各自让步,达成一致。
- We hope you can consider our counter offer and reply soon.
  希望您能考虑我们的还盘并早日回复。

Problems Solving

1. The following is a passage about counter offer. Fill in the blanks with the words given below.

| binding | response | implication | original | options |

Counter offer is an offer given in (1)_____ to an offer. It implies rejection of the (2)_____ offer and puts the ball back. The original offerer who has three (3)_____: to a) accept it, expressly or by (4)_____; b) issue another (counter-counter) offer, or c) reject it expressly. No (5)_____ contract can be created until one party accepts the other's offer.

2. Work in pairs to discuss the charges which are usually included in the quotation for freight forwarding services.

Section 4 Skills Training and Case Study Samples

Skills Training

A. There are ten incomplete sentences in this part. For each sentence there are three choices marked A, B and C. Choose the one that best completes the sentence.

1. Offer and _____ are elements required for the formation of a legally binding contract.

   A. realization   B. acceptance   C. reception

2. A firm offer should become binding as soon as it is accepted by the _____.

   A. offeror   B. offeree   C. offerer

3. An invitation to treat is an indication of a person's willingness to _____ a contract.

   A. negotiate   B. sign   C. discuss

4. An acceptance is a promise of an offeree indicating a willingness to be _____ by the terms and conditions contained in an offer.

   A. bound   B. carried   C. binding

5. You need to know more about the _____ before you make your offer.

   A. manager   B. customer   C. guest

6. Make sure you have all the tools available on your own end, including a good _____ and a dynamic website.

   A. brochure   B. manager   C. action

7. Your quotation should bear an identification _____ number and be clearly traceable from the customer's end.

   A. price   B. reference   C. quotation

8. Confirm the quantities which were requested and make clear that your prices are based on these _____.

   A. productions   B. conditions   C. volumes

9. Prices should be preferably in the _____ which was requested but make clear which prices belong to which quantities.

   A. share   B. create   C. currency

10. Prior investigation of the _____ of the customer may reduce the possible threats.

    A. credibility   B. situation   C. deduction

B. Translate the following terms into English.

询价   报价

实盘   还盘

参考号码   支付条件

产品手册   邀请发盘

账单   发货

C. Translate the following sentences into Chinese.

1. Making a quotation or an offer is a most important step in negotiating an export transaction.
2. An offer refers to a promise to supply goods on the terms and conditions stated.
3. When an offeree receives the offer, he/she may show disagreement to some terms such as price or payment terms in the offer.
4. A quotation is a reply to an inquiry, which is an offer in simple form including a notice of the price of certain goods being sold, but in no legal sense.
5. If an offeree disagrees with the relative terms in an offer, he/she may send a counter-offer to the offeror.

Case Study Samples

Sample 1

An Inquiry

An inquiry is a request for information on goods or services. When business people send out an inquiry, they may ask for a quotation or an offer for the goods or services they wish to get. An inquiry can be made by written correspondence, such as a letter, telegram, telex, fax, e-mail or verbally by talk in person.

Inquiries from regular customers may be very simple in content, in which only the name and/or specifications of the commodity will be mentioned. Other inquiries may include great details such as the name of the commodity, quality, specifications, quantity, terms of price, terms of payment, time of shipment, packing method, etc.

required by the buyer so as to enable the seller to make proper offers.

An inquiry received from abroad must be answered fully and promptly. If there is no stock available for the time being, you should acknowledge the inquiry at once, explaining the situation and assuring that you will reply to it once a supply becomes available. If the inquiry is from an old customer, express how much you appreciate it. If it is from a new customer, say you are glad to receive it and express the hope of a future business relationship. In a word, the reply to an inquiry should be prompt and courteous and cover all the information asked for.

 Problems Solving

1. What is an inquiry? What may be mentioned when you make an inquiry?
2. Suppose you have 200 dozens of Sports Socks to be delivered from Shanghai to New York. Write an inquiry to ABC International Transport Company asking for a quotation for freight forwarding services.

 Sample 2

ABC International Logistics Co., Ltd.
QUOTATION

20 GP-CIF

From Taishan, Guangzhou to the port of Miami, USA

Ocean vessel: CMD

	Expense Categories	Cost(CNY)
1	O/F: Ocean Fee	13600
2	ORC: Original Receiving Charges	1250
3	DOC: Document Charge	200
4	AMS: Automated Manifest System	300
5	ISPS: International Ship and Port Facility Security	200
6	Seal:	50
7	RRI: Rate Restoration Initiative	2090
8	Truck Haulage Charge:	2400(Factory Loading)
9	Customs Clearance Fee:	1100
10	Total:	21190
11	Weekly ETD:	Tuesday, From Shekou Port
12	Day:	30 days

 Problems Solving

1. Please translate the above quotation into Chinese.

2. Suppose you have received an inquiry from a new client who wants to deliver 1,000 pieces of Men's Shirts to Singapore. Write a quotation letter for your freight forwarding services. Your quotation should include the following:

(1) Thanks for the inquiry;

(2) The charges for freight forwarding services, the term of payment, and discounts;

(3) Hope for future cooperation.

Section 5　Elevating Vision and Useful Expressions

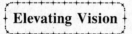

Freight Forwarding

Freight forwarding industry is an intermediary service industry between businesses and transport companies. A freight forwarder, forwarder, or forwarding agent, is usually a company that organizes shipments for individuals or corporations to get goods from the manufacturer or producer to a market, customer or final point of distribution. Forwarders contract with a carrier to move the goods. A forwarder does not move the goods but acts as an expert in supply chain management. A forwarder contracts with carriers to move cargo ranging from raw agricultural products to manufactured goods. Freight can be booked on a variety of shipping providers, including ships, airplanes, trucks, and railroads. It is not unusual for a single shipment to move on multiple carrier types. International freight forwarders typically handle international shipments. International freight forwarders have additional expertise in preparing and processing customs and other documentation and performing activities pertaining to international shipments. Some forwarders handle domestic shipments only.

Companies in this industry provide freight forwarding and customs brokerage services. Major companies include FedEx Trade Networks, UPS Supply Chain Solutions' and Sinotrans.

Demand is driven by domestic manufacturing output and levels of international trade. The profitability of individual companies depends on efficient operations, extensive relationships in shipper and carrier networks, and industry expertise. Large companies have advantages in account relationships and access to advanced logistics technologies.

Unlike fully integrated carriers that own truck, rail, air, or ocean assets and transport cargo, freight forwarders usually arrange the transportation of goods without owning any transportation equipment or handling the cargo. Customs brokers add another layer of expertise by facilitating the clearing of goods through international customs barriers. Most companies specialize in either freight forwarding or customs brokering, though they can provide both.

 Useful Expression

询价与议价用语	
a large demand 大的需求	F. A. S. (Free alongside Ship) 装运港船边交货
all in rate 全包价	F. C. A. (Free Carrier) 货交承运人
bill 账单	F. O. B. (Free on Board) 装运港船上交货
bring up goods fee 提货费	favorable price 优惠价格
buy single fee 买单费	firm offer 实盘
CFR (Cost and Freight) 成本加运费	for your reference/information 仅供参考
CIF (Cost, Insurance and Freight) 成本加保险加运费	price terms 价格条款
CIP (Carriage and Insurance Paid to) 运费、保险费付至	H/C (Handling Charge) 手续费/理货费
	handling and accessorial charges 货物处理及其他费用
CPT (Carriage Paid to) 运费付至	inbound service charges 进口服务费
cash 现金	increase 20% during legal festival 在法定节假日期间增加 20%
check 支票	
commercial inspect fee 商检费	insurance fee 保险费
consolidation fee 拼箱费	ISP (Inspection Charges) 检验费
counter offer 还盘	load and unload 装卸费
customs custody 监管费	M. T. (Metric ton) 公吨
customs fee 报关费	Min $20 per shipment 每票货最低收费 20 美元
D. A. P. (Delivered at Place) 目的地交货	
D. A. T. (Delivered at Terminal) 运输终端交货	net rate 成本费
D. D. P. (Delivered Duty Paid) 完税后交货	non-firm offer 虚盘
deat single fee 打单费	Per shipment 每票(货物)
debit note 收费账单	R. T. (Revenue Tons) 收费吨位
delivery charge 送货费	SCC (Switch Certificate Charges) 质检换证费
DOC Fee (Document Fee) 文件费	submit an offer 提交报盘
drayage charges 拖柜费	terminal handling charge (THC) 码头费用
entrance fee 仓租费	the complete stock 整批货
EXW (Ex works) 工厂交货	

Unit 2

Canvassion

Learning Objectives

- To know the roles a freight forwarder performs in international trade
- To know the scope of freight forwarding services
- To learn the key words and expressions in canvassing cargos

Skill Developing Objectives

- To develop communication skills in canvassing cargos
- To develop writing skills in establishing business relations

Section 1 Theme Lead-in

Read the following passage to get a better understanding of this unit.

How to Choose Your Freight Forwarder

How do you choose a freight forwarder to meet your needs? The most important is that the main objective of the freight forwarding company is to make sure customers receive the best freight services.

As a customer, you can benefit from:

- A combination of fair prices plus quality service is second to none. You can rely on a flexible and innovative approach in handling your freight needs.
- You're not just a consignment transaction and you are a respected customer with individual needs.
- A total distribution solution—whatever the commodity or service requirement, or destination, it will meet your needs.
- A contact for complementary services related to the shipment including packing, customs clearance, and bonded storage.
- An "easy to work with" approach for doing business. You will always be able to find out where your shipments are and you can reach your agent anytime.
- The support of well trained and motivated freight forwarders and logistics specialists.

If you are looking for a freight forwarder with complete services to handle your shipping needs and make the experience worry free, just find a company like this.

 Notes

1. The most important is that the main objective of a freight forwarding company is to make sure customers receive the best freight services.
   最重要的是货运代理公司的主要目标是确保顾客获得最好的货运服务。
2. A combination of fair prices plus quality service is second to none.
   合理的价格加上优质的服务无人可及。
3. You can rely on a flexible and innovative approach in handling your freight needs.
   对于货运需求,货运代理的服务不但灵活,而且具有创新性。
4. You're not just a consignment transaction and you are a respected customer with

individual needs.

你不仅仅是货物运输委托人，而且是一个受尊敬的有个性化需求的顾客。

5. A contact for complementary services related to the shipment including packing, customs clearance, and bonded storage.

货运合同包括与运输相关的补充性服务，如包装、海关清关、保税仓储等。

6. The support of well trained and motivated freight forwarders and logistics specialists.

能够获得受过良好训练，积极主动的货运代理人及物流专家的支持。

Problems Solving

1. Work in pairs to discuss how to choose a good freight forwarder.
2. Decide whether the following statement is true or false according to the passage.

（1）The main objective of a good freight forwarder is to make profit. （   ）

（2）You can benefit a combination of fair prices plus quality service from a good freight forwarder. （   ）

（3）A good freight forwarder can offer complementary services related to the shipment. （   ）

（4）Freight forwarders should be trained and motivated. （   ）

（5）A good freight forwarder doesn't offer individual services. （   ）

Section 2　Conversations and Warm-up

Conversations

Conversation 1　Introduction to a Freight Forwarding Company

(A is Li Hong, a receptionist of a freight forwarding company, who is talking with B, Liu Jing, a potential client from Sichuan Machinery Imp. & Exp. Corporation.)

A: Welcome to our company. What can I do for you?

B: Good morning. I am Liu Jing from Sichuan Machinery Imp. & Exp. Corporation. Could you give me a brief introduction to your company?

A: Sure. Our company is one of the leading freight forwarders in China and our business covers import and export container transportation and agency, warehousing, door to door pick-up and delivery, customs clearance and consolidation.

B: I see. Do you have any famous customers?

A: We have had good business relationship with Cinki Company in your area for ten years. You can refer to Cinki Company for more information about our company.

B: I will. Do you have your own warehouse?

A: Yes, of course. We have more than 80,000-square-meter warehouse spaces.

B: Oh, it's very impressive! Thank you for your information.

A: You are welcome. If you have any logistics questions, please don't hesitate to ask me. We have a reputation for top service.

B: I will. Thank you.

 Conversation 2 Discussing Transportation Means

(*B is Mr. Edward, who is discussing transportation means with his shipper A, who wants to explore the possibility of transshipment due to shipping congestion.*)

A: Mr. Edward, we were just informed that lately there has been much congestion in shipping. There are very few direct steamers sailing for your port. So is there any chance if transshipment is allowed?

B: Well, transshipment will prolong the delivery and is likely to cause damage. So, we still hope a direct shipment could be arranged.

A: Now the trouble is that it is very difficult to book shipping space. I'm afraid we can do little about this.

B: You surely know that transshipment adds to the expenses and sometimes may delay the arrival. If the goods can not be put on the market on time, then good quality and competitive price would mean nothing.

A: Yes, we really understand your position. Anyhow, we'll try. We'll see whether we can get the cooperation of the China National Chartering Corporation. It has a good reputation for meeting the client's varied demands.

B: Thank you very much indeed.

 Conversation 3 Complaining Delay of an Order

(*A, Mr. Cook is from Shenyang Chemical Imp. & Exp. Co.,Ltd. complains about the delay of an order with B, who works in Tianjin Ocean Shipping Corp.*)

B: We've checked the delivery order, and it should have reached you last Friday. I'm so sorry about that.

A: You know we supply the materials for a manufacture company; our work cannot be late with the materials. Our customer has been affected because of the delay.

B: Sorry, Sir. We promise you will get it next Monday.

A: What if we don't get it by then? Our manager isn't satisfied with your service. This is our first order with your company, and things like this shouldn't have happened.

B: I fully understand your position at this moment. This will never happen again. I do hope this incident won't affect our future business relations.

A: Well, I hope so.

 Warm-up

A. Match the definitions in Column B with the terms in Column A.

A	B
1. logistics	A. a part that has express or implied authority to act for another
2. cargo	B. a person whose work consists of supporting management, including executives
3. agent	C. the management of the flow of things between the point of origin and the point of consumption
4. carrier	D. all articles or goods carried onboard an aircraft, ship, train or truck
5. secretary	E. a company that transports goods by air, land, or sea in its own or chartered vessels

B. The following is a passage about business relations. Fill in the blanks with the words given in the box and then discuss with your partners about the roles a freight forwarder performs in international trade.

| carrier   dispatch   logistics   destination   documentation |

A freight forwarder (often just forwarder) is a third party (1) _____ provider. As a third party (or non asset based) provider, a forwarder (2) _____ shipments via asset based carriers and books or otherwise arranges space for those shipments. (3) _____ types include Ocean Cargo Ships, Airplanes, Trucks or Railroad. Freight forwarders typically arrange cargo movement to an international (4) _____. Also referred to as international freight forwarders, they have the expertise that allows them to prepare and process the (5) _____ and perform related activities pertaining to international shipments.

C. Make up a conversation according to the following situation.

Student A works as a receptionist in a logistics company, and Student B is a client who is looking for a freight forwarder to deliver his goods. Student A and Student B will act out the dialogue of establishing business relations.

The dialogue should cover the following information: greeting, an introduction to the freight forwarding company, and the intention to establish business relations.

Section 3　Format Writings and Practical Usages

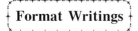

After reading the following passage, you are required to discuss with your partners and to complete the statements that follow the questions.

Introduction Letter

A letter aiming at establishing business relations is usually essential and useful. An introduction letter consists of the following steps:

Where you get the information about the person or company to whom you are writing the letter;

The information can be obtained through trade fairs and exhibitions held at home and abroad, through the introduction of business partners, banks or advertisements.

Your intention for establishing business relations;

Courtesy is necessary when you express your writing intention, which is to introduce yourself and intend to have a good impression on the partners.

A brief introduction of your business scope, experience, products or services;

A complete letter should include the introduction about the scope of business activities. It is better if the writer could enclose products brochure and price list.

The reference as to your firm's credit standing if necessary;

As firms involved in business may be located in different countries, it is necessary to introduce the firm's credit standing to others. In addition, your partner would refer to financial status and reliability from banks, such as Bank of China.

Expectation for cooperation and an early reply.

The most commonly used sentence is: We look forward to your favorable reply.

 Problems Solving

1. What is the useful and essential way to establish business relations?

2. How many steps when you write an introduction letter?
3. What are the possible channels to get the name and address of a firm?
4. What should be noted when you intend to introduce your firm?
5. Why does a firm want to know the partners' credit standing?

 Writing Samples

Letter 1 Self-Introduction

May 15, 2024

Dear Sir,

We are writing to introduce ourselves as one of the leading logistics companies in China and we would be greatly honored if you could appoint us to be your freight forwarder in China.

Our company was established in 1996 and has been involved in international container freight forwarding business for almost 30 years. As a Class Alicense holder with full authorization from the government, we can conduct space booking, customs brokerage and other related services. We pride ourselves as one of the first logistics companies in Shanghai to launch full line of services including logistics services, bonded warehouse facility, project cargo handling, city-pair trucking service, etc.

We are willing to enter into business relations with your company on the basis of equality and mutual benefit.

Yours faithfully,

Letter 2 Establishing Business Relations

May 21, 2024

Dear Sir,

Through the courtesy of Mr. Freeman, we are given to understand that you are one of the leading freight forwarders in your area. We would like to appoint your company to be our general agent for the liner service from China to the Persian Gulf ports.

We look forward to receiving your acceptance of this offer and establishing direct business relations with you at an early date. The management of our whole operations is undertaken by OOCL, our local branch in your area. In connection with detailed business to handle henceforth, please contact directly our local branch offices concerned.

We are looking forward to our close cooperation and business development in the future.

Yours faithfully,

Practical Usages

1. Self-Introduction 自我介绍

1) To introduce oneself
   介绍自己

- We are writing to introduce ourselves as one of the leading logistics companies in China and we would be greatly honored if you could appoint us to be your freight forwarder in China.
  我公司是中国物流行业龙头企业,若贵公司指定我方作为中国地区货运代理,我们将深感荣幸。

2) To introduce business scope
   介绍业务范围

- Our company was established in 1996 and has been involved in international container freight forwarding business for almost 30 years.
  我公司成立于1996年,从事国际集装箱货运代理业务已近30年。

- As a Class A license holder with full authorization from the government, we can conduct space booking, customs brokerage and other related services.
  我公司是经政府认证的A类企业,可提供订舱、代理报关和其他相关服务。

- We pride ourselves as one of the first logistics companies in Shanghai to launch full line of services including logistics services, bonded warehouse facility, project cargo handing, city-pair trucking service, etc.
  我公司是上海首批提供全程服务的物流公司,可提供物流服务、保税区仓储、项目货物和城际托运服务等,为此我们深感自豪。

2. Establishing Business Relations 建立业务关系

1) To mention the source of information
   提及获知信息的渠道

- Through the courtesy of Mr. Freeman, we are given to understand that you are one of the leading freight forwarders in your area.

承蒙 Freeman 先生介绍，我方得知贵公司是你方地区货运代理的龙头企业。

- Thanks to ABC Company for recommending your company to us.

  承蒙 ABC 公司向我方推荐了贵公司。

2) To express the intention to establish business relations

   表达对建立业务关系的期待

- We are willing to enter into business relations with your company on the basis of equality and mutual benefit.

  我们愿意在平等互利的基础上与贵公司建立业务关系。

- We would like to appoint your company as our general agent for the liner service from China to the Persian Gulf ports.

  我方愿意委托贵公司作为本公司中国到波斯湾班轮航线的中国总代理。

3) To mention the services

   提及服务

- In connection with detailed business to handle henceforth, please contact directly our local branch offices concerned.

  今后各项具体业务事宜，请直接与我公司下属的有关当地分公司联系。

- At present, we are interested in the service offered by your company and would like to have your catalogues and quotations.

  目前我们对贵公司提供的服务很感兴趣，希望获得贵方的服务目录与报价。

Problems Solving

1. The following is a letter for promoting business relations. Fill in the blanks with the words given below.

enclosed   appointment   assure   provided   appreciated   perusal

Dear Sir,

Thank you for your letter of May 21, 2024 and we are pleased to confirm our acceptance of your (1)_____ to act as your general agents in China for your liner service.

We (2)_____ herewith two booklets, The Business Regulations of China Ocean Shipping Agency and Charges and Rates of China Ocean Shipping Agency, for your (3)_____. Our agency business transactions are to follow the same, (4)_____ you have no objection to them. Your confirmation of your agreement to the above will be highly (5)_____.

We wish you every success of your business and (6)_____ you of our closest attention to the commitments.

Yours sincerely,

2. Suppose you are a canvasser in a freight forwarding company. Write a letter to a potential client to express your intention to establish business relations.

Section 4　Skills Training and Case Study Samples

Skills Training

A. There are ten incomplete sentences in this part. For each sentence there are three choices marked A, B and C. Choose the one that best completes the sentence.

1. To _____ business relations with prospective dealers is very important for a company.
   A. establish　　　B. offer　　　C. make

2. Our company can provide different _____ of transportations.
   A. measures　　　B. means　　　C. approaches

3. We have special _____ on long-term contract.
   A. permissions　　　B. concessions　　　C. discussions

4. An introduction letter should include the content about the _____ of business activities.
   A. quotation　　　B. catalogue　　　C. scope

5. We would be greatly honored if you could _____ us to be your freight forwarder.
   A. appoint　　　B. mention　　　C. deliver

6. Our company can conduct space booking, customs _____ and other related services.
   A. support　　　B. brokerage　　　C. contract

7. We are willing to enter _____ business relations with your company.
   A. by　　　B. against　　　C. into

8. Our company's main _____ is to make sure customers receive the best freight services.
   A. objective　　　B. operation　　　C. production

9. As a customer, you can benefit from the _____ prices offered by our

company.

    A. average   B. fair   C. fine

10. You can get the support of well trained and _____ freight forwarders.

    A. liable   B. motivated   C. respective

B. Translate the following terms into English.

货运代理　　　　　　　建立业务关系

龙头企业　　　　　　　潜在客户

随函附上　　　　　　　产品目录

报价单　　　　　　　　业务范围

物流行业　　　　　　　代表

C. Translate the following sentences into Chinese.

1. With the development of modern economy, people are more and more aware of the importance of logistics.
2. Every company that sells products has to need the service of logistics.
3. Our company has become one of the market leaders in China's freight forwarding industry.
4. As a representative of ABC Company, I hope to establish business relations with you.
5. If you are concerned about logistics questions, please do not hesitate to ask me.

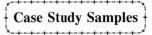

 Sample 1

An Introduction to DHL

    DHL is present in over 220 countries and territories across the globe, making it the most international company in the world. With a workforce exceeding 325,000 employees, we provide solutions for an almost infinite number of logistics needs.

    DHL is part of the world's leading postal and logistics company Deutsche Post DHL Group, and encompasses the business units DHL Express, DHL Parcel, DHL e-Commerce, DHL Global Forwarding, DHL Freight and DHL Supply Chain.

    DHL provides you ocean freight shipping services. The professional staff at DHL is prepared to ship your freight to or from anywhere in the world. Whether your cargo is shipping overseas or within the United States coastline, we consider your freight our main concern. DHL has expanded its resources to ensure that the most reliable and dependable vessels will be transporting your ocean freight.

Shipping Containers Available:
Full Container Loads (FCL)
20 Foot Container
40 Foot Container
45 Foot High-Cube Container
Specialized Equipment (available upon request)
Less Than Container Loads (LCL)
20 Foot Flat-Beds or Flat-Racks
40 Foot Flat-Beds or Flat-Racks

We handle varied types of cargo:
- Machinery
- Heavy Equipment
- Generators
- Industrial Machinery
- Break Bulk

Allow us the opportunity to service your ocean freight needs. We'll provide a detailed estimate with competitive ocean freight rates.

Problems Solving

1. Do you know DHL? Make a three-minute presentation to introduce DHL. You can use some visual aid to help you to express yourself, such as a flowchart, a diagram or a PPT.
2. Suppose you work as a canvasser in Marketing Department of DHL. Write an introduction letter to a new client to establish business relations.

Sample 2

Investigation Report

On establishing business relations with another company, a company must conduct careful investigation before entering into such relationship. The investigation related with the company's business scope and credit standing must be done. The employee appointed to do investigation work should write a report. The following is a good example:

Report on Kelong International Transportation Co., Ltd.

To: ABC Company
From: Shirley Smith
Date: March 6, 2024

Introduction

Kelong International Transportation Co., Ltd. was founded in 1994 and has become one of the leading companies in China's freight forwarding and logistics industry. The research and development activities are conducted at its headquarters. The Purpose of this report is to provide you with financial data necessary to force your decision about establishing relations and to offer my recommendations.

Findings

Kelong prides itself as a Class A license holder and one of the first companies in China to be awarded the ISO 9001/9002 certificates. Kelong provides full line of services including import and export multiple transportations, door to door pickup and delivery, customs clearance, bonded warehousing, etc. In 2023, the operating revenue of Kelong was up to 1.65 billion CNY. The customer/auditor complaint ratio was 120 people and damage ratio was 0.025%.

Conclusions and Recommendations

The company's financial position is clearly very strong. It has experienced a steady growth in freight forwarding industry. It is my opinion, therefore, that it is very wise to enter into business relations and to maintain a long-term relationship with Kelong Company.

 Problems Solving

1. If you are required to write a similar report, what should you pay attention to?
2. Do you think it is wise to build up good relations with Kelong Company? Why? Write a letter to Kelong Company to express your intention to establish business relations.

 # Section 5 Elevating Vision and Useful Expressions

> **Elevating Vision**

Freight Forwarding Services List

The following is a list of services that a freight forwarder on behalf of the consignor (exporter) and the consignee (importer).

On Behalf of the Consignor (Exporter):

- Choose the route, mode of transport and a suitable carrier.
- Book space with the selected carrier.
- Take delivery of the goods and issue relevant documents such as the Forwarders' Certificate of Receipt (FCR), the Forwarders' Certificate of Transport (FCT), etc.
- Study the provisions of the letter of credit (L/C) and all Government regulations applicable to the shipment of goods in the country of export, the country of import, as well as any transit country; he would also prepare all the necessary documents.
- Pack the goods, taking into account the route, the mode of transport, the nature of the goods and applicable regulations, if any, in the country of export, transit countries and country of destination.
- Arrange warehousing of the goods, if necessary.
- Weigh and measure the goods.
- Draw the consignor's attention to the need for insurance and arrange for the insurance of goods, if required by the consignor.
- Transport the goods to the port, arrange for customs clearance, related documentation formalities and deliver the goods to the carrier.
- Attend to foreign exchange transactions, if any.
- Pay fees and other charges including freight.
- Obtain the signed bills of lading from the carrier and arrange delivery to the consignor.
- Arrange for transshipment if necessary.
- Monitor the movement of goods all the way to the consignee through contacts with the carrier and the forwarders' agents abroad.
- Note damages or losses, if any, to the goods.
- Assist the consignor in pursuing claims, if any, against the carrier for loss of the goods or for damage to them.

On Behalf of the Consignee (Importer):

- Monitor the movement of goods on behalf of the consignee when the consignee controls freight, that is, the cargo.
- Receive and check all the relevant documents relating to the movement of the

goods.
- Take delivery of the goods from the carrier and pay the freight costs.
- Arrange customs clearance and pay duties, fees and other charges to the customs and other public authorities.
- Arrange transit warehousing, if necessary.
- Deliver the cleared goods to the consignee.
- Assist the consignee, if necessary, in pursuing claims, if any, against the carrier for the loss of the goods or any damage to them.
- Assist the consignee, if necessary, in warehousing and distribution.

 Useful Expression

接单揽货用语	
advertisement 广告	image 形象
appoint 指派	investigation 调查
brochure 小册子,宣传册	joint venture enterprise 合资企业
business relations 业务关系	make offers 报盘
business scope 业务范围	market share 市场份额
cargo canvassing 揽货	marketable 适销的
catalogue 目录	mutual 共同的
chamber of commerce 商会	pamphlet 小册子,手册
channel 渠道	potential 潜在的
client 客户	quotation 报价
cooperate 合作	receipt 收据
corporation 公司	recommendation 推荐
credit standing 资信状况	reliability 可靠性
customer 顾客	reputation 声誉
enclose 附上	specialize in 专营
exhibition 展览会	specific 特有的
FIATA (International Federation of Freight Forwarders Associations) 国际货运代理协会联合会	state-owned enterprise 国有企业
	transaction 业务
financial position 财务状况	WCA (World Cargo Alliance) 世界货运联盟

Unit 3

Warehousing and Chartering Space

Learning Objectives

- ➢ To know the main functions of warehousing
- ➢ To understand the procedure of warehousing operation
- ➢ To learn the key words and expressions in warehousing

Skill Developing Objectives

- ➢ To develop communication skills in introducing the warehouse
- ➢ To develop writing skills in introducing the warehouse

Section 1   Theme Lead-in

Read the following passage to get a better understanding of this unit.

Warehouse Operations

Warehouses are operated in several ways. Public warehousing involves the client paying a standard fee for the storage of merchandise. Private warehousing is storage and operations controlled completely by a single manufacturer. Contract warehousing clients pay fees regardless of whether they are using the space or not; the space is always there for them to use, however. According to "An Overview of Warehousing in North America", contract warehousing accounts for more than 60% of the U. S. commercial market.

A warehouse stands empty without some form of product. Delivery of goods and materials takes place either by truck, rail, or boat on a dock or loading area. The goods are received, processed, and then sent into the warehouse for storage.

The storage of goods has been the primary function for warehouses. Once the goods have been received from the manufacturer and/or shipper, they are compactly stored to maximize space within the facility. Products are placed on pallets, which allow for more consistent stacking and moving within the facility.

Contract and public warehouses receive goods and products from a multitude of manufacturers and shippers. A crucial aspect of warehouse management is inventory control. Inventory control is the ability to locate and track a given product within the warehouse to facilitate quick selection and loading for order fulfillment. It is also the process of maintaining sufficient amounts of product to meet customer demands, while at the same time balancing the expense of keeping product in storage. Perpetual, annual, physical, and cycle counting are all methods of keeping track of inventory.

Warehousing is also involved in the packaging and labeling of a product as it moves through the facility. Proper packaging is necessary for effective storage and to guard against damage. Labeling, or tagging, is an important element of the packaging. Proper labeling improves the ability to identify, track, store, and select the correct product for order fulfillment.

Once the product has been selected, or picked, it is brought to a staging area for final processing and shipment. The loading dock is a hub of activity as products are arriving for storage and being staged for distribution. Effective management of this area is crucial for warehouse success. It is here that cross-docking takes place.

The final stage of warehousing is the transportation facet of delivering and shipping goods.

Notes

1. Public warehousing involves the client paying a standard fee for the storage of merchandise.
   在公共仓储中,顾客储存货物需要按标准支付费用。

2. Contract warehousing clients pay fees regardless of whether they are using the space or not; the space is always there for them to use, however.
   合同仓储的顾客不管是否使用了仓库,都需要支付费用。但是这能保证仓库会随时供他们使用。

3. According to "An Overview of Warehousing in North America", contract warehousing accounts for more than 60% of the U. S. commercial market.
   根据"北美仓储概述",合同仓储占美国商业市场的60%以上。

4. Delivery of goods and materials takes place either by truck, rail, or boat on a dock or loading area.
   商品和原材料的交付是在码头或装载区由卡车、铁路或者轮船来完成。

5. Once the goods have been received from the manufacturer and/or shipper, they are compactly stored to maximize space within the facility.
   来自厂家和(或者)托运人的商品一旦被接收,就会紧凑储存以最大化利用仓储空间。

6. Products are placed on pallets, which allow for more consistent stacking and moving within the facility.
   产品置于托盘上以便整齐堆垛和运输。

7. Inventory control is the ability to locate and track a given product within the warehouse to facilitate quick selection and loading for order fulfillment.
   库存控制是定位和跟踪仓库某一特定产品的能力,以提高快速分拣和装载速度来处理订单。

8. It is also the process of maintaining sufficient amounts of product to meet customer demands, while at the same time balancing the expense of keeping product in storage.
   它还指在平衡储存产品费用的同时,能够保持足够产品量以满足顾客需求的过程。

9. Perpetual, annual, physical, and cycle counting are all methods of keeping track

of inventory.

跟踪库存的方法包括永续盘存、年度盘点、实物盘点、循环盘点。

10. Warehousing is also involved in the packaging and labeling of a product as it moves through the facility.

当产品通过仓库时,仓储还包括产品包装和贴标签。

11. Proper labeling improves the ability to identify, track, store, and select the correct product for order fulfillment.

合适的标签能够提高识别、跟踪、存储、拣取正确产品以处理订单的能力。

12. Once the product has been selected, or picked, it is brought to a staging area for final processing and shipment.

产品一旦被分拣,就送到物流中转区准备最后处理和装运。

13. The loading dock is a hub of activity as products are arriving for storage and being staged for distribution.

装货月台是产品送达后进行储存和配送时的活动中心。

 Problems Solving

1. Fill in the blanks with the words given in the box.

standard	staging	temporary	labeling	desired

(1) Usually, warehouses are typically viewed as a _____ place to store goods.

(2) Warehousing plays a vital role in providing a _____ level of customer services.

(3) Clients of a public warehouse need to pay a _____ fee for the storage of merchandise.

(4) The products are brought to a _____ area for final processing and shipment once they have been selected.

(5) Warehousing is also involved in the packaging and of _____ a product.

2. What types of warehouse are mentioned in the passage?

3. Could you make a brief introduction about the functions of a warehouse?

 # Section 2　Conversations and Warm-up

+-+-+-+-+-+-+-+-+
: **Conversations** :
+-+-+-+-+-+-+-+-+

 Conversation 1　Visiting a Warehouse

(B is showing A round the warehouse, and A takes the advantage to get to know *how warehouse is operated on daily basis.*)

A: Thank you for taking your time to give a tour around the warehouse. I have a question here: Do all warehouses serve the same purpose?

B: According to the storage purpose, there can be three types of warehouse, deliver-center, storage-center and logistics-center.

A: How do you handle the goods after they arrive at the warehouse?

B: First indoor operation, then warehouse management, finally warehouse operation.

A: What is indoor operation?

B: A series procedures includes arranging warehouses, checking the goods, enrolling the goods accurately, loading and depositing them in standard.

A: What about the warehouse management?

B: We need to check the products and facilities regularly, keep the warehouse clean and safe, standardize each operation and gather the information.

A: Then warehouse operation?

B: It means providing the goods according to the shipment list, and save and file the bills of document.

 Conversation 2   Talking About the Goods in a Warehouse

(*A is Daniel, a manager in a logistics company, who is talking with B, Kenny, a warehouse keeper.*)

A: Kenny, how come these few cartons of goods without placing any label?

B: Let me see… these goods are just unloaded from a container.

A: You should have labeled them before carrying them into store, in case the workers have mixed them with the goods from other customers.

B: Yes, I'll pay attention to it.

A: Who do they belong to?

B: If I'm not mistaken, they belong to Mr. Smith from Beijing Enterprise Co., Ltd.

A: Did he have any instruction of the way for placing his goods?

B: No, he just informed us the date of unloading and the quantity of goods.

A: Check with Mr. Smith to see if these cartons can be palletized. If yes, move them to Section A immediately. It will save a lot of space.

 Conversation 3   Introducing the Work in a Warehouse

(*A is John, a warehouse keeper, who is talking with B, Wang Lin, a*

newcomer.)

A: Nice to meet you. I'm the warehouse keeper, John.

B: Nice to meet you. I'm Wang Lin. Could you briefly introduce the procedures after the goods arrive at the warehouse?

A: Sure. First indoor operation, then warehouse management, and finally warehouse operation.

B: What is indoor operation?

A: They are a series of procedures including arranging storehouses, checking the goods, enrolling the goods accurately, loading and depositing them in standard.

B: What about the warehouse management?

A: We need to check the products and facilities regularly, keep the warehouse clean and safe, standardize each operation and gather the information.

B: And what's the warehouse operation?

A: It consists of five aspects: the warehouse procedures, the quantity of the goods, loading the goods and depositing them in standard, providing the goods according to the shipment list, saving and filing the bills of document.

B: Wow, you are so great! It's very important to be a warehouse keeper. I got it. Thank you very much!

 Warm-up

A. Match the definitions in Column B with the terms in Column A.

A	B
1. inventory	A. a key part of the supply chain and primarily aims to control the movement and storage of materials within a warehouse
2. WMS (warehouse management system)	B. a very large metal or wooden box used for transporting goods so that they can be loaded easily onto ships and lorries
3. receiving space	C. a detailed list of all the items in stock
4. container	D. a flat wooden or metal platform on which goods are stored so that they can be lifted and moved using a forklift truck
5. pallet	E. the area for unloading goods in warehouse

B. The following is a passage about warehouse. Fill in the blanks with the words given in the box and then discuss with your partners on what a warehouse is.

| forklifts   trucks   storage   manufacturers   seaports |

A warehouse is a commercial building for (1) _____ of goods. Warehouses are used by (2) _____, importers, exporters, wholesales, transport businesses, customs, etc. They are usually large plain buildings in industrial areas of cities and towns. They usually have loading docks to load and unload goods from (3) _____. Sometimes warehouses load and unload goods directly from railways, airports, or (4) _____. They often have cranes and (5) _____ for moving goods, which are usually placed on ISO standard pallets loaded into pallet racks. Stored goods can include any raw materials, packing materials, spare parts, components, or finished goods associated with agriculture, manufacturing and production.

C. Make up a dialogue according to the following situation.

Student A works as a warehouse keeper in a logistics company, and Student B is a client who is visiting the warehouse. Student A and Student B will act out a dialogue about the warehouse.

The dialogue should cover the following information: greeting, an introduction to the warehouse, and the warehouse keeper's work.

Section 3　Format Writings and Practical Usages

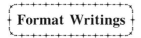

After reading the following passage, you are required to complete the statements that follow the questions.

Warehousing and Warehouse Functions

Warehousing is the storage of goods for profit. The physical location, the warehouse, is a storage facility that receives goods and products for the eventual distribution to consumers or other businesses. Warehouse management is the process of coordinating the incoming goods, the subsequent storage and tracking of the goods, and finally, the distribution of the goods to their proper destinations.

Warehousing is a key component of the overall business supply chain. The supply chain consists of the facilities and distribution options for the procurement of materials from manufacturer to customer and all points in between. It includes the production of materials into components and finished products and then the distribution to customers.

Warehousing companies are now striving to become more than simply storage facilities. They are transforming themselves into "third-party logistics providers" or

"3PLs" that provide a wide array of services and functions. In addition to packing and staging pallets, contemporary warehousing facilities offer light manufacturing, call centers, labeling, and other non-storage options.

Warehouse functions include:
- the storage of goods to permit managing product flow or to accommodate longer production runs;
- serving as a mixing point where products from different suppliers are mixed and then distributed to fulfill customer orders;
- a sales branch and customer service location;
- a source of supplies for production;
- a staging area for final packaging or finishing.

 Problems Solving

1. According to the passage, what is warehouse management?
2. What does a business supply chain consist of?
3. What does "3PLs" refer to?
4. What is a modern warehousing company like?
5. What are the functions of a warehouse?

 Writing Samples

Letter 1   Renting Warehouse Space

May 16, 2024

Dear Mr. Smith,

Further to our discussion last week in which I outlined our need for warehousing over the next eighteen months, I would like to enquire if the warehouse space is still available at the W1 site.

We would have the following requirements:
- 24-hour access;
- must have security;
- adequate parking for twenty and easy access.

Thank you for your attention, and I look forward to your prompt reply.

Yours sincerely,

Letter 2　Business Proposal

May 17, 2024

Dear Mr. Burr,

　　Further to your enquiry about the warehousing at the W1 site, I am delighted to say that the space is still available. However, with regard to your additional requirements please note that you would have to rent two separate spaces of 50 square meters and the warehouse has limited parking for five cars only and limited access.

　　As an alternative, you might wish to consider a new storage option called Circular Storage that has recently become available to customers. While it is a little further from the centre of the city than W1, it has the following features:

　　- easy access for lorries and adequate parking for twenty;

　　- security with CCTV;

　　- space availability of 100 square meters (and more if required).

　　Please also note that it would be two-thirds the price of W1, and the 10% discount for a two-year booking would apply.

　　I look forward to hearing from you in the very near future.

Yours sincerely,

 Practical Usages

1. Renting Warehouse Space 租用仓库

Mention your intention to renting warehouse space

表明租用仓库的意向

- I would like to enquire if the warehouse space is still available at the W1 site.
  我们想咨询下目前W1仓库是否还可以租用？
- We are wondering that whether we can rent the warehousing space for twelve months?
  我们想知道仓库是否可以租用12个月？

2. Business Proposal 商务建议

1) Replying the inquiry

　　回应询问

- Further to your enquiry about the warehousing at the W1 site, I am delighted to say this space is still available.

就您所询问的位于 W1 的仓库,我很高兴地告诉您仍可租用。

- Please note that you would have to rent two separate spaces of 50 square meters and the warehouse has limited parking for five cars only and limited access.

  请注意您要租两个 50 平方米的场地,仓库只有 5 个停车位,禁止随便进入。

2) Introducing the proposal

  提出建议

- As an alternative, you might wish to consider a new storage option called Circular Storage that has recently become available to customers.

  作为备选,您也许可以考虑近期向顾客开放的仓储地 Circular Storage。

- Maybe you can consider a warehouse about one mile from the W3.

  也许您可以考虑另一个仓库,距离 W3 大约 1 英里。

3) Providing reasons/Comparing pros and cons

  给出理由/比较优劣

- It has the following features:

  -easy access for lorries and adequate parking for twenty;

  -security with CCTV;

  -space availability of 100 square meters (and more if required).

  它具有下列特点:

  -卡车出入方便,足有 20 个停车位;

  -闭路电视安保系统;

  -100 平方米的可用仓储空间(如果需要可以提供更大的空间)。

4) Balancing and concluding

  权衡与结论

- Please also note that it would be two-thirds the price of W1, and the 10% discount for a two-year booking would apply.

  请注意租金是 W1 仓库的三分之二,租用两年可以打九折。

- Please consider this possibility and the discount would still apply if you rent our new warehouse.

  请考虑这种可能性。如果租用我们的新仓库,折扣仍然有效。

Problems Solving

1. The following is a reply to the requirements of a client who wants to rent a warehouse. Fill in the blanks with the words given below.

Warehousing and Chartering Space
Unit 3

| discount | bookings | space | consider | availability | square |

Dear Mr. Rice,

Thank you for your order by fax. Further to your request for warehousing (1)_____ for twelve months, I'd like to mention that I can also offer you a 10% discount for (2)_____ of an eighteen-month period.

You enquired about (3)_____ at the W3 site, but we are very regret that there is no any space available. Maybe you can (4)_____ our new warehouse called Dockside (about one mile down the riverside from the W3). It has the space availability of 100 (5)_____ meters.

Please consider this possibility and note the (6)_____ would still apply. A visit to this warehouse can be arranged, although I would suggest a prompt decision on this second option.

I look forward to hearing from you in the very near future.

Yours sincerely,

2. Write an e-mail to your customer, introducing your warehouse and hoping to establish business relations.

Section 4   Skills Training and Case Study Samples

Skills Training

A. There are ten incomplete sentences in this part. For each sentence there are three choices marked A, B and C. Choose the one that best completes the sentence.

1. Most organizations arrange for stocks to be kept in _____.

    A. warehouses   B. containers   C. pallets

2. Traditionally warehouses were seen as places for the long-term storage of goods. Now organizations try to move materials quickly through the supply chain, so their _____ has changed.

    A. importance   B. role   C. type

3. In general, the aims of a warehouse are to _____ the broader logistics function by giving a combination of high customer service and low costs.

    A. support   B. influence   C. compete

4. For small organizations owning their own warehouses would be both difficult

and _____, so they use facilities provided by specialized warehousing companies.

  A. cheap   B. possible   C. expensive

  5. The _____ of a warehouse describes the physical arrangement of storage racks, loading and unloading areas, equipment, offices, rooms, and all other facilities.

  A. layout   B. location   C. purpose

  6. Automatic warehouses need a very high investment in _____, and are only really worthwhile for very big stores that move large amounts of materials.

  A. activity   B. strategy   C. equipment

  7. A warehouse is the general term for any place where materials are stored on their journey through a(n) _____.

  A. production   B. organization   C. supply chain

  8. The traditional warehouse involves a range of activities from receiving materials for _____, through to preparing deliveries for customers.

  A. processing   B. storage   C. sorting

  9. A _____ warehouse is run as an independent business, which makes money by charging users a fee.

  A. public   B. private   C. sorting

  10. Stocks occur at any point in the supply chain where the _____ of materials is interrupted.

  A. storage   B. flow   C. assembling

B. Translate the following terms into English.

入库作业   核对物品
登记   装货月台
贴标签   托盘
分拣   跟踪库存
自营仓库   储存

C. Translate the following sentences into Chinese.

1. Warehousing is the link between producers and consumers.
2. Our business covers import and export container transportation and agency, door to door pickup and delivery, warehousing and consolidation.
3. Our company can provide customers with a variety of goods inventory, such as raw material, semi-finished products, finished products, spare parts, etc.
4. Warehousing is not a new business, but it has gained new functions in modern

logistics.
5. Setting inventory levels requires downstream information from customers on demand, upstream information from suppliers on availability and information on current inventory levels.

+ Case Study Samples +

 Sample 1

Daniel West Wholesale

Daniel West Wholesale (DWW) is a privately owned wholesaler of frozen fish and a range of fresh foods. It employs 85 people, receives goods from 52 suppliers, and delivers to 570 main customers in the north of England using a fleet of 26 vans. All its operations are based in a single warehouse in Gateshead.

DWW is successful in a highly competitive market, and it attributes its success to its outstanding customer service. This is judged by the five criteria of close personal relationships, flexibility to respond to individual needs, low prices enhanced by discounts, high stocks meeting 98% of orders off the shelf, and frequent deliveries, normally twice a day.

DWW's turnover is £35 million a year, with a gross margin of about 4.5%. All the costs are classified as acquisition (76%), storage (7%), distribution (4%) and others (13%).

Every morning the order-processing room in DWW checks orders that have been automatically sent by customer tills, e-mailed, faxed, or telephoned overnight. Then they contact customers who have not sent orders, asking if they want anything. These orders are consolidated into "customer requirement lists", which are sent to the warehouse. The goods for each order are picked from the shelves, assembled, put into a delivery box, checked, and taken to a departure bay. At the departure bay the materials have final packing and promotional material added.

The customer requirement lists are used to design routes for the vans. The drivers collect the schedule of customers to be visited, pick up the boxes to be delivered, and load them into the van in the specified order. Then they set off on their deliveries, visiting an average of 20 customers, traveling 110 miles a morning, and delivering £3,000 of goods. This whole procedure is repeated on a slight smaller scale in the afternoon.

After each of the main delivery runs, DWW's purchasing system analyses the purchases, consolidates these into orders, and automatically transmits them to suppliers.

 Problems Solving

1. Why is DWW successful in a highly competitive market? What can we learn from its success?
2. What roles does the warehouse play in DWW?

 Sample 2

Warehousing and Distribution in DHL

By understanding your issues and anticipating your business and logistics needs, DHL experts provide robust solutions that will drive value for your business. Whatever industry sector you operate in, DHL provides dedicated and shared warehousing and distribution operations to ensure that you can deliver your service promise to your customers worldwide.

We offer every combination of warehousing solution that your supply chain might require, including:

- Ambient
- Temperature-controlled
- Bonded
- Raw Materials
- Finished Goods
- Automated

DHL can offer you a variety of automated systems within its warehouse offering, all of which are designed to bring significant efficiencies to your operations. Every order that moves through DHL freight system is assigned a reference number that is used to track and trace the order from time of pick up to ultimate delivery at destination.

DHL has a continued commitment to service. Our fully computerized shipment management system ensures the accuracy and consistency required in today's fast-paced shipping environment.

 Problems Solving

1. Do you think DHL offers excellent warehousing and distribution services? Why?

2. Suppose you are a warehouse manager in DHL. Make a three-minute presentation to introduce the warehouse. You can use some visual aid to help you to express yourself, such as a flowchart, a diagram or a PPT.

Section 5   Elevating Vision and Useful Expressions

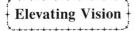

25 Canadian Forces Supply Depot

25 Canadian Forces Supply Depot opened in Montreal in 1995. This 60,000 square meter warehouse replaced three earlier facilities in Montreal, Toronto and Moncton. Its aim is to receive, warehouse and issue everything needed to support bases, stations, ships and service battalions across eastern Canada and United Nations peacekeeping units around the world.

The warehouse receives new materials from commercial suppliers and returns from Canadian Forces units. When a truck arrives, the documents are checked and the vehicle is directed to one of 11 receiving docks. There it is unloaded, bar codes on materials are scanned, and data is fed into the warehouse management information system (WMIS). Materials are then put onto conveyors, where each unit is automatically weighed and measured. When everything has been checked, and details confirmed, the materials are officially "received". Then WMIS prints a "license plate" bar code to identify each unit, and assigns a storage location. This location is set by the features of the unit, and is chosen to give the best use of storage space. WMIS then delivers the unit to its storage location, using fixed, hand-held and vehicle-mounted scanners around the warehouse to track and control movements. WMIS is also linked to other Canadian Forces systems to keep track of ordering, stocks, invoicing and related information.

WMIS has four different types of storage location:
- Larger, palletized shipments are moved by forklift from the conveyor to one of six stacker cranes which work in the high bay area. There are 18 aisles, 20 meters high, providing 140,000 locations for storage.
- Smaller units are taken from the conveyor by a monorail system which delivers them to the mid-rise stacks. Four monorail trains, each with eight trolleys, move on a 400 meter track and take units to delivery chutes. They are picked up

- by 10 wire-guided stock pickers which work in the 37 aisles, 10 meters high, providing 600,000 storage locations.
- Larger units are taken from a special arrivals dock to the bulk storage area, which has space six meters high for freestanding goods.
- Hazardous materials are taken from a special arrivals dock to a separate area for special treatment.

 Useful Expression

仓 储 用 语	
article reserves 物品储存	handing/carrying 搬运
automatic guided vehicle (AGV) 自动导引车	humidity controlled space 控湿储存区
automatic warehouse 自动化仓库	inventory control 库存控制
boned warehouse 保税仓库	joint distribution 共同配送
box car 箱式车	loading and unloading 装卸
chill space 冷藏区	order cycle time 订货处理周期
container transport 集装箱运输	order picking 拣选
containerization 集装化	palletizing 托盘包装
conveyor 输送机	pallet 托盘
crane 起重机	receiving space 收货区
cross docking 直接换装;交叉配送	safety stock 安全库存
distribution center 配送中心	shipping space 发货区
distribution processing 流通加工	sorting 分拣
export supervised warehouse 出口监管仓库	stacking 堆码
fork lift truck 叉车	stereoscopic warehouse 立体仓库
freeze space 冷冻区	storehouse 库房
goods collection 集货	temperature controlled space 温度可控区
goods shed 料棚	unit loading and unloading 单元装卸
goods shelf 货架	warehouse layout 仓库布局
goods stack 货垛	

Unit 4

Packaging

Learning Objectives

- To know the functions packaging performs in logistics process
- To learn the main types of packaging
- To learn the key words and expressions of packaging

Skill Developing Objectives

- To develop communication skills in dealing with packaging
- To develop writing skills in the negotiation of packaging

Section 1   Theme Lead-in

Read the following passage to get a better understanding of this unit.

Packaging

In recent years, packaging has become an important industry. Packaging is the end of the production process and the beginning of the logistics process. Packaging is to seal the products with materials, containers and auxiliary items so that the products can be distributed to the consumer in the safety way. One of the basic purposes of packaging is to protect the products in the good condition. The other purpose of packaging is to promote the sales. Packaging provides the information between the manufacturer and consumer. It can appeal the consumer to buy according to the packaging information. Consumer can judge the products according to the information provided by packaging, so the insufficient packaging can affect sales.

Packaging has three methods: Nude cargo refers to the goods that can remain its original form and resist external impact in the certain natural conditions, which can be packaged, such as steel bars, steel sheets and timber. Bulk cargo refers to bulk, low-cost, powder-like goods. Bulk cargo does not have to be packaged, which are loaded loosely into carriage, for instance, coal, grain, and petroleum. Piece items are the general name for finished goods, packaged or un-packaged. Piece items are again classified into single-piece shipment packing and integrated shipment packing. Single-piece shipment packaging includes cases, drums, bags, bales, bundles. The packaging materials including wooden cases, cartons, iron drums, gunny bags, and plastics bags have to be marked. Integrated shipment packaging includes flexible containers, pallet, and container.

Packaging is divided into consumer packaging and industrial packaging according to the purpose. The main purpose of commercial packaging is to promote sales, which appeals the customers and is regarded as the interior packaging. The customers can find the commercial packaging on the shop shelf. Elegant shapes, necessary decorations and structure are the main characteristics for the commercial packaging. In addition, interesting picture, and bright color can also appeal the customers to buy. The main purpose of industrial packaging is to protect the produces in the logistics process. This package is discarded before the products are placed on the shelf, so the customers can never see this material. In the process of the industrial packaging, we should find the optimal balance between the packaging cost and the loss happened in the transportation.

The function of packaging can be summarized up in the following: To protect and preserve the products from damage during handling, storing and transportation. When package is being transported, we cannot avoid the damage caused by vibration, impact, puncture and compression. The packaging can promote logistic efficient, which can reduce the waste. If the packaging is designed efficiently in the logistics processing, the integrated logistics system will be benefited. The size, shape and type of packaging material will have influence on the type and amount of material handling equipment.

Notes

1. Packaging has become an important industry. Packaging is the end of the production process and the beginning of the logistics process.
   包装成为很重要的一门产业。包装是生产过程的最后一个环节,也是物流过程的开始。

2. Packaging is to seal the products with material, containers and auxiliary items so that the products can distribute to the consumer in the safety way.
   包装是用材料、容器和其他辅助的东西,使产品以安全的方式分配给消费者。

3. One of the basic purposes of packaging is to protect the products in the good condition.
   包装最基本的作用就是保护商品。

4. The other purpose of packaging is to promote the sales. Packaging provides the information between the manufacturer and consumer.
   包装还有个用途就是促进销售,包装在生产者和消费者之间提供信息。

5. Consumer can judge the products according to the information provided by packaging, so the insufficient packaging can affect sales.
   消费者可以根据包装提供的信息判断商品,因此包装对销售有直接的影响。

6. Nude cargo refers to the goods that can remain its original form and resist external impact in the certain natural conditions.
   裸装货主要是指在一定的自然条件下能抵抗外在影响,不需要包装的货物。

7. Bulk cargo does not have to be packaged, which are loaded loosely into carriage.
   散装的货物不需要包装,一般被散放在车里。

8. Piece items are again classified into single-piece shipment packing and integrated shipment packing.
   件货又分为单件运输包装和集合运输包装。

9. The packaging materials including wooden cases, cartons, iron drums, gunny bags, and plastics bags have to be marked.

   包括木箱子、纸板箱、铁桶、麻布袋、塑料袋等在内的包装材料需要标明。

10. Integrated shipment packaging includes flexible containers, pallet, and container.

    集合运输包装有弹性集装袋、托盘、集装箱等。

11. Packaging is divided into the consumer packaging and industrial packaging according to the purpose.

    根据用途,包装分为消费包装和工业包装。

12. The main purpose of commercial packaging is to promote sales, which appeals the customers and is regarded as the interior packaging.

    商业包装以促销为主要目的,这种包装主要是吸引顾客,为内包装。

13. To protect and preserve the products from damage during handling, storing and transportation.

    包装主要是保护商品,防止在搬运、存储和运输过程中破损。

14. The packaging can promote logistic efficient, which can reduce the waste.

    包装可以提高物流效率,减少浪费。

15. If the packaging is designed efficiently in the logistics processing, the integrated logistics system will be benefited.

    如果包装在物流过程中设计得很有效果,那么就会起很大作用。

Problems Solving

1. What are the purposes of packaging?
2. What is the difference between consumer packaging and industrial packaging?
3. The following is the definition of packaging. Fill in the blanks with the words given below.

| protecting | storage | process | coordinated | logistics |

Packaging is the technology of enclosing or (1) _____ products for distribution, (2) _____, sale, and use. Packaging also refers to the (3) _____ of design, evaluation, and production of packages. Packaging can be described as a (4) _____ system of preparing goods for transport, warehousing, (5) _____, sale, and end use.

Section 2　Conversations and Warm-up

Conversations

 Conversation 1　Types of Packaging

(*B is Mr. Jones, who is negotiating with his consignor A about what kind of packaging is most suitable for the present consignment.*)

A: Mr. Jones, shall we now discuss the packaging?

B: Very well. You know, we have definite ways of packaging garments. As to blouses, we use a polythene wrapper for each article, all ready for window display.

A: Good. A wrapping that catches the eye will certainly help push the sales. With competition from similar garments producers, the merchandise must not only be good value but also look attractive.

B: Right you are. We'll see to it that the blouses appeal to the eye as well as to the purse.

A: What about the outer packing?

B: We'll pack them 10 dozens to one carton, gross weight around 25 kilos a carton.

A: Cartons?

B: Yes, corrugated cardboard boxes.

A: Could you use wooden cases instead?

B: Why use wooden cases?

A: I'm afraid the cardboard boxes are not strong enough for such a heavy load.

B: The cartons are comparatively light, and therefore easy to handle. They won't be stowed away with the heavy cargo. The stevedores will see to that. Besides, we'll reinforce the cartons with straps. Silk blouses are not fragile goods. They can stand a lot of jolting.

 Conversation 2　Methods of Packaging

(*A is Mr. Zhang, who is speaking with B, Fred Wilson. They are continuing their talks about packaging.*)

A: Good morning. May I help you?

B: Good morning. This is Fred Wilson from Wanda Company. Could you tell me if we pack the coal, how should we do?

A: You do not need to pack the coal. The coal belongs to bulk cargo.

B: What is bulk cargo?

A: Bulk cargo refers to bulk, low-cost, powder-like goods, for example, coal, grain, and petroleum. Bulk cargo does not have to be packaged, which are loaded loosely into carriage.

B: We also hear the nude cargo, and can you introduce more information for us?

A: Nude cargo refers to the goods that can remain its original form and resist external impact in the certain natural conditions, which can be packaged, such as steel bars, steel sheets and timber.

B: Can you give us some recommendations about liquids packaging?

A: Liquids are packed in tins, which are very popular in the world market. Many leading companies of beverage, such as Coca Cola, they pack their liquids in tins. I think you can use the similar packaging ways to pack, and incorporate an opener on the top of each tin.

B: What about foot wears?

A: We introduce the cartons to pack, the cartons are lined with waterproof plastic sheets, and it is handled with care.

B: Thank you for your recommendation, and we will consider.

A: You are welcome.

 Conversation 3　Functions of Packaging

(*A is Mr. Zhang, and B is Fred Wilson from Wanda Company. They are continuing their talks about packaging.*)

A: DHL. Can I help you?

B: This is Fred Wilson from Wanda Company. We have already chosen the sea voyage for our cargo. What should we pay more attention to in the packaging?

A: You should protect and preserve the products from damage during handling, storing and transportation.

B: Why do we choose carton instead of wooden case?

A: The charge for that kind of packaging will be higher, and it also slows down delivery.

B: What is the benefit for the right packaging?

A: The packaging can promote logistic efficiency, which can reduce the waste. The size, shape and type of packaging material will have influence on the type and amount of material handling equipment.

B: If the product is potentially dangerous, what we should do?

A: If the product is potentially dangerous, such as liquid and fireworks, the packaging should provide instructions for avoiding moisture, heating and vibration.

B: Thank you very much.

A: You are welcome.

 Warm-up

A. Match the definitions in Column B with the terms in Column A.

A	B
1. nude cargo	A. interior or marketing package which appeals the customers
2. bulk cargo	B. the goods can remain its original form and resist external impact in the certain natural conditions
3. wrapper	C. commodity cargo that is transported unpackaged in large quantities
4. commercial package	D. exterior package, which is discarded before the products are placed on the shelf
5. industrial package	E. a type of packaging, such as a flat sheet made out of paper

B. The following is a passage about packaging. Fill in the blanks with the words given in the box and discuss with your partners about the importance of packaging.

packing   destination   arrival   specific   attach

As packing materials used and the ways the goods are packed will, to some extent, determine whether the goods can reach the (1) _____ in sound condition, the exporter should (2) _____ importance to the packing of the goods. On the part of the seller, he should ensure that the (3) _____ can effectively protect the foods from damage and can sustain the long distance of transport. For the buyer, the punctual (4) _____ of goods in perfect condition is of great importance, so he may have (5) _____ packing requirements. If so, he should inform the exporter of them before shipment.

C. Make up a dialogue according to the following situation.

Student A works as a clerk in East Shipping Company, and Student B is a client who is willing to know how to package the goods to be exported. Student A and Student

B will act out the dialogue about packaging.

The dialogue should cover the following information: greeting, an introduction to the material of package, and the intention to cooperate.

Section 3   Format Writings and Practical Usages

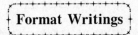

After reading the following passage, you are required to discuss with your partners and to complete the statements that follow the questions.

Packaging Materials

The most common types of material used for packaging are paper, board, plastic, glass, steel and aluminum.

Paper and board are the most widely used packaging materials. They account for 43% of all packaging.

Plastic packaging accounts for 20% of all packaging. Because of its low weight, plastic is one of the most energy efficient, robust and economic delivery methods available.

Glass accounts for 20% of all packaging. Glass can be recycled easily. Well established collection and recycling systems exist in many countries because they have a developed collection infrastructure.

Aluminum is used to make beverage and food cans, foils and laminates. It has a high value as a scrap metal and can be recycled economically. Steel containers are used to package a wide range of products, including food, paint and beverages as well as aerosols.

 Problems Solving

1. According to the passage, how many types of material are used for packaging?
2. What kind of material is the most widely used?
3. Why is plastic one of the most energy efficient, robust and economic delivery methods available?
4. What is the advantage of glass used for packaging?
5. What kinds of metal material can be used for packaging?

Writing Samples

Letter 1 Negotiation on Carton Packing

May 6, 2024

Dear Sirs,

We are pleased to have received your letter of May 5, in which you mentioned to pack the 28,000 raincoats in wooden cases.

According to our comparative study of the characteristics of carton packing and wooden case packing, as well as the results of shipments already made, we recommend you pack the raincoats in cartons instead of in wooden cases, as packing in cartons has the following advantages.

(1) It will prevent skillful pilferage, for the traces of pilferage will be more in evidence.

(2) It is fairly fit for ocean transportation.

(3) Our cartons are well protected against moisture by plastic lining.

(4) Cartons are comparatively light and compact, so they are more convenient to handle.

We hope you will accept our carton packing and assure you of our sincere cooperation.

Yours faithfully,

Letter 2 Importer Accepts Modes of Packaging

May 12, 2024

Dear Sir,

Thank you for your letter of May 6, recommending us to pack the raincoats in cartons.

In reply we are now confirming the acceptance of your modes of packing, for packing in cartons can prevent skillful pilferage, and cartons lined with polythene sheets are well protected against moisture and are comparatively light and compact.

Please note that the raincoats shall be packed in a polythene bag each and then in a cardboard box, 12 dozen to a carton, with a gross weight of some 38 kilograms. Each carton is secured by overall strapping thus preventing the possible damage in transit.

We trust that the above instructions are clear to you and that the shipment will give the users entire satisfaction.

Sincerely yours,

Letter 3 Packing Instruction

Oct. 25, 2024

Dear Sir,

We appreciate your e-mail asking about packaging types. As our products are easily damaged, it is quite necessary to pay special attention to packaging. Frankly speaking, our packaging requirements are quite strict. The details are written in our packing instruction, which is attached. However, I'd like to emphasize the following four points:

1. The packaging must be strong enough to withstand rough handling.

2. The products are to be wrapped in double canvas before being packed in cartons.

3. The most important thing is to protect the goods from vibrations.

4. Any loss in transit is to be compensated by your company.

We believe you will give special care to the packaging to avoid any possible damage, for which we really appreciate.

Yours faithfully,

Practical Usages

1. Negotiation on Packing 协商包装

1) To mention the previous letter

提及上封来信

- We are pleased to have received your letter of May 5, in which you mentioned to pack the 28,000 raincoats in wooden cases.

  很高兴收到你方 5 月 5 日的来信,信中提及 28,000 件雨衣用木箱包装。

- Thank you for your letter of July 12 and for your interest in our packaging services.

  感谢你方 7 月 12 日来信,并对我方的包装服务感兴趣。

2) To persuade to receive the packaging
   劝说接受包装样式
- We recommend you pack the raincoats in cartons instead of in wooden cases, as packing in cartons has the following advantages.
  我们建议你方用纸箱包装雨衣,而不是用木箱,因为纸箱有以下优势。
- It will prevent skillful pilferage, for the traces of pilferage will be more in evidence.
  它可以防止偷窃,因为更容易发现偷窃的证据。
- Cartons are comparatively light and compact, so they are more convenient to handle.
  纸箱相对轻,而且紧凑,因此更容易搬运。

3) To express the expectation for cooperation
   表明合作的意愿
- We hope you will accept our carton packing and assure you of our sincere cooperation.
  我们希望你方能接受纸箱包装,并向你方保证我方的合作诚意。
- We trust you will find our packaging satisfactory and look forward to your next cooperation.
  我们相信你会非常满意我们的包装,期待下次合作。

2. Packing Instruction 包装指示

1) To mention the previous letter
   提及上封来信
- We appreciate your e-mail asking about packaging types.
  我方感谢你方关于包装方式的邮件。
- Thank you for your packing suggestion related to these products.
  非常感谢你对这类产品的包装建议。

2) To state the packaging requirements and explain the reasons
   说明包装要求并解释原因
- Please note that the raincoats shall be packed in a polythene bag each and then in a cardboard box, 12 dozen to a carton, with a gross weight of some 38 kilograms.
  请注意每件雨衣需用聚乙烯袋包装,然后装入纸板盒中,每12打一个纸箱,毛重38千克。
- Each carton is secured by overall strapping thus preventing the possible damage

in transit.

每个纸板箱用皮带捆绑，以防运输中可能的损坏。

- As our products are easily damaged, it is quite necessary to pay special attention to packaging.

  我们的产品容易损坏，因此需要在包装上特别用心。

- The products are to be wrapped in double canvas before being packed in cartons.

  在装入纸箱之前，产品必须用双层帆布包装。

- The packaging must be strong enough to withstand rough handling.

  包装必须结实，经得住粗鲁的搬运。

- All the cases must be lined with waterproof paper, and Please mark the bales with our Initials ABC.

  所有的箱子都必须有防水包装，并在箱子上打上 ABC。

- The products packed in wooden cases are susceptible to damage by moisture, and the batch number should be marked on each container.

  这些产品用木头箱子包装很容易受潮，每个箱子上面都应该有批号。

- This product should be packed in international standard box according to the usual practice.

  根据以往的惯例，这个产品应该用国际标准的盒子包装。

Problems Solving

1. Fill in the blanks with the words given below.

batch	packed	standard	suitably	withstand

（1）The product will be _____ in wooden cases.

（2）The packing must be strong enough to _____ rough handling.

（3）Consumer goods must be packed _____ and attractively to reinforce company's image in the market.

（4）The product should be packed in international _____ box.

（5）The _____ number should be marked on each container.

2. Suppose you are a freight forwarder. Write an e-mail to your client to give some suggestions about packaging. In your e-mail, the following information should be included：

（1）Thanks for his e-mail you received yesterday；

（2）The materials to be used for package and the methods of packaging；

（3）To express the expectation for cooperation.

Section 4 Skills Training and Case Study Samples

Skills Training

A. There are ten incomplete sentences in this part. For each sentence there are three choices marked A, B and C. Choose the one that best completes the sentence.

1. Packaging is divided into the commercial packaging and _____ packaging.
   A. neutral   B. sale   C. industrial

2. _____ is the end of the production process and the beginning of the logistics process.
   A. Transporting   B. Packaging   C. Chartering

3. Elegant shapes, necessary decorations and structure are the main characteristics for _____.
   A. commercial packaging   B. industry packing   C. transport packing

4. _____ is to protect the products in the logistics process.
   A. Commercial packaging   B. Industry packing   C. Interior packing

5. _____ refers to the goods such as steel bars, steel sheets and timber.
   A. Nude cargo   B. Bulk cargo   C. Piece items

6. _____ refers to bulk, low-cost, powder-like goods.
   A. Nude cargo   B. Bulk cargo   C. Piece items

7. _____ are packing in the tins, which are very popular in the world market.
   A. Timber   B. Liquids   C. Wood

8. Integrated shipment packaging includes flexible containers, pallet and _____.
   A. box   B. cartons   C. container

9. The function of packaging is _____.
   A. to facilitate the handling ease
   B. to protect and preserve the products
   C. to transfer the information

10. Packaging is to seal the products with _____, containers and auxiliary items so that the products can distribute to the consumer in the safety way.
    A. canvas   B. plastic   C. material

B. Translate the following terms into English.

销售包装   集装箱

工业包装　　　　　纸箱
防水　　　　　　　包装材料
内包装　　　　　　外包装
内衬　　　　　　　裸装货

C. Translate the following sentences into Chinese.

1. These goods didn't sell well merely because of the poor packing.
2. The packing must be strong enough to withstand rough handling.
3. Thanks to packaging it is possible for products to be available anytime anywhere that gives the consumer a great freedom of choice.
4. Transport packaging is also called outer packaging, which means packaging designed to facilitate handling and transport of a number of sales units or grouped packaging in order to prevent physical damages.
5. Shipping mark contains identification mark, identification number, and total number of items in the complete consignment, and also the place and port of destination.

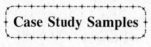

Sample 1

Packaging Advice

Our company is committed to delivering your shipments with speed and care. Shipments are handled frequently as they pass through many facilities across the world. In order to make sure your shipments arrive in the best possible condition, here are packaging tips and helpful advice on preparing your shipment.

Consider Content Size and Packaging Options
- Under-filled boxes may collapse.
- Overloaded boxes may burst.
- Do not exceed the weight specification of the shipment container.

Boxes
- Boxes are the most commonly used and suitable way to pack your shipment because of the range of sizes, shapes, materials and accessories to strengthen and secure them.

- Wood containers are especially appropriate for shipping heavier items and are ready for machine handling.
- Heavy-duty double-layered cardboard is a suitable and cheaper alternative to wood boxes.

Envelopes
- Use cardboard envelopes for lightweight documents.
- Use cushioned, padded or bubble envelopes to carry things like discs, tapes, keys and small electronic parts.
- Waterproof and anti-static versions are also available.
- Do not use envelopes made of fabric.

Flyers
- Our own branded flyer bags are available in two sizes:
  - Standard Flyer: For flat documents and small binders with a maximum weight of 2 kg;
  - Large Flyer: For flat documents, ring binders and small boxes with a maximum weight of 3 kg;
- Flyers should always be used when the shipment is smaller than an industry standard shipping label or waybill.

Tubes
- Use triangular tubes instead of round tube-type cylinders for rolled items.
- Round tubes roll—which makes them difficult to handle.
- Round tubes cannot pass through the automated sorting equipment generally used in our sorting facilities.
- Our triangular tubes are specially designed to ship maps, blueprints and any type of large flexible document and are available in two sizes for up to 2 kg or 5 kg.

Problems Solving

1. How many types of packaging are mentioned in the passage? What are they?
2. If you want to pack some large machines, what method of packaging will you choose? Why?
3. Make a presentation to introduce the advantage and disadvantage of each type of packaging mentioned in the passage. You can use some visual aid to help you to express yourself, such as a flowchart, a diagram or a PPT.

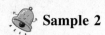 **Sample 2**

Packaging Design

Packaging is more than just your product's pretty face. Your package design may affect everything from breakage rates in shipment to whether stores will be willing to stock it. The original slanted-roof metal container used for Log Cabin Syrup was changed to a design that was easier to stack after grocers became reluctant to devote the necessary amounts of shelf space to the awkward packages. Other distribution-related packaging considerations include:

Labeling. You may be required to include certain information on the label of your product when it is distributed in specific ways. For example, labels of food products sold in retail outlets must contain information about their ingredients and nutritional value.

Opening. If your product is one that will be distributed in such a way that customers will want to—and should be able to—sample or examine it before buying, your packaging will have to be easy to open and to reclose. If, on the other hand, your product should not be opened by anyone other than the purchaser—an over-the-counter medication, for instance—then the packaging will have to be designed to resist and reveal tampering.

Size. If your product must be shipped a long distance to its distribution point, then bulky or heavy packaging may add too much to transportation costs.

Durability. Many products endure rough handling between their production point and their ultimate consumer. If your distribution system can't be relied upon to protect your product, your packaging will have to do the job.

 Problems Solving

1. What are the packaging strategies in this passage?
2. What is shipping mark? Surf the internet for the key elements that a shipping mark consists of and try to design a shipping mark.

 # Section 5　Elevating Vision and Useful Expressions

+ Elevating Vision +

Optimal Packaging

Optimal packaging of a product is a critical factor in logistics. And the reason is clear: without it, many logistics processes could not be performed at all or could be carried out only at great additional cost. The function of the packaging is not just to protect the product. It performs many other jobs as well. These include providing information about the contents as well as enabling and facilitating other logistics processes-including transport and handling as well as storage, order processing and warehousing.

The different logistics functions of the packaging—that is, protection, storage, transport, information and handling—are an outstanding example of the interdependencies that exist in logistics. As a result, the packaging may be regarded only as a part of the entire logistics system. In packaging design, a compromise that addresses all functional areas must be found. The correct design of packaging can help lower overall logistics costs and raise the level of supply and/or delivery service. In addition to the logistics functions, packaging must also fulfill production functions, marketing functions and usage functions.

Through the choice of suitable packaging, it is possible to produce directly from the packaging or into the packaging without intermediary processing procedures.

Packaging can lend a special character to a product, enabling it to be distinguished from the competitors' products. Important functions can also be assigned to packaging, including roles in advertising and sales promotions.

In light of environmental considerations, it is essential for packaging design to meet these needs. Ideally, the design should make it possible for a customer to recycle the packaging or facilitate its use for other purposes.

- Protective function

   Good service includes the ordered good's arriving in satisfactory condition. The packaging should protect the product from mechanical and climatic stresses during delivery.

- Warehouse function

   Packaging is required to facilitate the storage of a product. If possible, the packaging should be stackable and meet the demands of the storage equipment. In addition, it should facilitate practical storage of the packaging supplies.

- Transportation function

   The packaging also has the task of facilitating the transport of a product or actually enabling the product to be transported. Likewise, the packaging's form and size should permit the optimal use of the transport space with the lowest possible packaging weight.

- Handling function

The goods should be combined by the packaging into units that simplify their processing during transshipment and delivery. The form and size of the packaging units must also facilitate the employment of technical aids such as forklifts or storage and retrieval systems. If the commodity is handled manually, then grip holes in the packaging can be necessary.

- Information function

The packaging should be marked in such a way that the products in it can be identified easily. Furthermore, packaging of fragile, perishable or similar products requiring special treatment during delivery should be clearly marked with pictures, symbols or explanations. During automated transportation and processing procedures, automatic product recognition is facilitated by suitable information.

 Useful Expression

包 装 用 语	
adhesive tape 胶带	gross weight 毛重
bale 包	handle with care 小心轻放,小心装运
barrel 桶	heave here 起吊点(此处起吊)
blister packing 起泡包装	hogshead 大桶
bulk pack 整批包装	in block 块装
bundle 捆	in bulk 散装
canvas 帆布	in bundle 捆(扎)装
carton 纸箱	in nude 裸装
case 箱	in slice 片装
centre of balance 重心	in spear 条装
consumer pack 零售包装	inflammable 易燃品
container 集装箱	iron drum 铁桶
cylinder 铁桶	jute bag 麻袋
drum 圆桶	keep away from moisture 防潮
explosive 爆炸品	keep flat/stow level 必须平放
fermented plastic 泡沫塑料	keep in hold 装于舱内
fiber board case 纤维板箱	keep on deck 甲板装运
fragile 易碎	keep upright 请勿倒置

Continued

包 装 用 语	
lift here 由此吊起	sack 袋
net weight 净重	saw dust 木屑
neutral packing 中性包装	seaworthy packing 适合海运包装
not to be tipped 请勿倾倒	shipping mark 运输标志,唛头
nude packing 裸装	skin packing 吸塑包装
nylon plastic 尼龙丝	sling here 挂绳位置
open from this side 由此开启	stuffing material 填料
packing capacity 包装容积	tar paper 沥青纸
packing mark 包装唛头	tare weight 皮重
packing number 包袋件数	use rollers 用滚子搬运
paper scrap 纸屑	waterproof paper 防水纸
plastic bag 塑料袋	wax paper 蜡纸
point of strength 着力点	wooden case 木箱
rate 板条箱	zippered bag 拉链袋

Unit 5

Loading

Learning Objectives

- To know the procedure of loading
- To know the main modes of goods transportation
- To learn the key words and expressions in loading

Skill Developing Objectives

- To develop communication skills in dealing with loading
- To develop writing skills in dealing with loading

Section 1 Theme Lead-in

Read the following passage to get a better understanding of this unit.

Making the Shipment

Shipment means that the seller fulfills his obligation to load goods into the named carrier at the given place and the time stipulated in the contract.

The buyer and the seller should reach an agreement on time of shipment, port of shipment and port of destination, shipping advice, partial shipment and transshipment, dispatch and demurrage, etc., and specify them in the sales contract.

Clear stipulation of the shipment clause is an important condition for the smooth execution of the contract. The consignor, carrier and consignee are the three parties involved in the shipment of goods. Shipment covers rather a wide range of work, such as booking shipping space, chartering ships, making customs declaration, etc.

Before shipment, the buyers generally send their shipping requirements to the seller, informing them in writing of the packing and marking, mode of transportation, etc. and the sellers should send shipping advice to the buyers immediately after the goods are loaded onboard the ship, advising them of the shipment.

The shipment clauses include the time of shipment, the ports of loading and destination, modes of transportation and the shipping documents.

Time of shipment refers to the time limit for loading the contracted goods on the collecting vehicle or placing the goods at the disposal of the carrier. Exporter must not advance or delay shipment. In case of a violation of the shipment term by the exporter, the importer may reject the goods, withdraw the contract and at the same time claim for compensation.

When stipulating the time of shipment, both parties should consider: the availability of goods, ships and shipping space, the issuing date of L/C and the nature of the cargo. Avoid ambiguous phrases like "immediate shipment", "prompt shipment", "shipment as soon as possible" and so on.

As for the port of shipment and port of destination, there are some issues worth noticing. Generally, one specific port of shipment and one particular port of destination are stipulated. On some occasions, two or more ports of shipment and ports of destinations are named. Sometimes, several alternatives of ports can be listed.

There are many means of transportation, and each has its advantages and drawbacks. Goods can be transported by a train, a truck, a plane, a ship or through a pipeline. The method used depends on time and cost. The Ocean Marine transportation has its own advantages of large holding capacity and low freight, so in spite of its disadvantages of slow navigation speed and strong risks, it still makes up over two-thirds of total freight volume of the transportation in international trade. Container transport also called containerization, is a method of distributing merchandise in a unitized form thereby permitting an inter-modal transport system to be evolved providing a possible combination of rail, road, canal and maritime transport.

Partial shipments and transshipment also belong to the kinds of shipments. It is necessary to instruct in the contract and in the L/C whether transshipment or partial shipments are checked and to observe these stipulations strictly.

In L/C checking, these stipulations should be checked carefully and the checking of how many partial shipments needs to be effected and the dates of these partial shipments should not be left.

Shipping advice is a note usually sent by the seller to inform the buyer that the goods he has ordered have been dispatched on ship. It gives a detailed description of the goods sent including the name of the ship, the date of shipping, name of the goods, its quantity as well as its specifications. Sending the shipping advice on time is the seller's responsibility stated in the contract. But if the seller neglects it, or forgets to notify the buyer, the buyer has no right to refuse the bill of lading. A bill of lading is a cargo receipt made out by the ship owner. It is the evidence of a contract of carriage between the consignor and the shipping company.

 Notes

1. Shipment means that the seller fulfills his obligation to load goods into the named carrier at the given place and the time stipulated in the contract.
   装运是指买方根据合同规定的地点和时间履行义务将货物装入指定的船上。
2. The buyer and the seller should reach an agreement on time of shipment, port of shipment and port of destination, shipping advice, partial shipment and transshipment, dispatch and demurrage, etc., and specify them in the sales contract.
   买方和卖方应该就装运期、装运港、目的港、装运通知、是否分批装运和转船、调度和滞期费等问题达成一致,并在销售合同中写明。
3. Clear stipulation of the shipment clause is an important condition for the smooth

execution of the contract.

清楚地订明装运条款,对于合同的顺利履行至关重要。

4. Time of shipment refers to the time limit for loading the contracted goods on the collecting vehicle or placing the goods at the disposal of the carrier.

装运时间是指卖方将合同规定的货物装上运输工具或交给承运人接管的期限。

5. Shipping advice is a note usually sent by the seller to inform the buyer that the goods he has ordered have been dispatched on ship.

装船通知是指卖方在货物装船后发出的一种通知。

6. It gives a detailed description of the goods sent including the name of the ship, the date of shipping, name of the goods, its quantity as well as its specifications.

其内容包括载货船名、装船日期、货物名称、数量、规格等。

7. Sending the shipping advice on time is the seller's responsibility stated in the contract.

在进出口双方签订的合同条款下,无延误地发出装船通知是卖方必须履行的义务。

8. Container transport also called containerization, is a method of distributing merchandise in a unitized form thereby permitting an inter-modal transport system to be evolved providing a possible combination of rail, road, canal and maritime transport.

集装箱运输是一种组合式的货物发送方式。这种交互式的货运系统结合了铁路运输、陆路运输、运河运输以及海上运输等货运方式。

9. A bill of lading is a cargo receipt made out by the ship owner. It is the evidence of a contract of carriage between the consignor and the shipping company.

提单是承运人出具的作为承运货物的收据,是代表承运人和托运人之间的运输合同。

Problems Solving

1. What should be considered when stipulating the time of shipment?

2. Decide whether the following statement is true or false.

(1) The sellers should send shipping advice to the buyers immediately after the goods are loaded onboard the ship. ( )

(2) The phrases like "immediate shipment" should be avoided when stipulating the time of shipment. ( )

(3) Two parties are involved in the shipment of goods. They are consignor and consignee. ( )

(4) Shipping advice is a note usually sent by the buyer. ( )

(5) A bill of lading is a cargo receipt made out by the seller. ( )

Section 2　Conversations and Warm-up

Conversations

  Conversation 1　Determining Port of Loading

(*A is Mr. Wang, a transportation operator of Fast Freight Forwarder, who is speaking with B, Mr. Zhang, an exporter.*)

A: Fast Freight Forwarder. What can I do for you?

B: This is Zhang Jun from ABC Company. We will export 10,000 foot wears from Shanghai to Africa. Since you are our general agents, we would like to discuss the port of loading with you.

A: We haven't decided yet. But we are thinking of taking Shanghai as the loading port. Do you have any specific requirements?

B: Perfect. It's better to designate Shanghai as the loading port since all the goods are produced there and it's easier to load at the port.

A: No problem. In that case, the shipment becomes much easier. Is there anything else?

B: No. Thank you for your understanding. I think our cooperation would bring both of us great interest.

A: That's for sure.

  Conversation 2　Urging Prompt Delivery

(*A is Mr. Smith, the manager of Shipment Department in Fast Freight Forwarder, who is speaking with B, Mr. Zhang, an exporter.*)

A: Fast Freight Forwarder. May I help you?

B: Yes. I would like to speak to Mr. Smith, the manager of Shipment Department.

A: Speaking, please. What can I do for you?

B: This is Zhang Jun from ABC Company. Can you make prompt delivery on our goods? We hope you can effect shipment in October.

A: I really hate to disappoint you. But your goods are too big, we cannot deliver the whole lot in such a short time, since it takes time to make out the documents and booking the shipping space.

B: How about partial shipment? You can ship whatever you are ready in the early part of October.

A: Partial shipment? Let me see. Oh, it is a good idea. We can ship the first half of your goods in the early part of October.

B: That's excellent. But I hope you won't make transshipment of our goods, because transshipment adds expenses as well as risk of damage and pilferage.

A: Okay, no problem.

B: Thank you.

 Conversation 3 Giving Shipping Instructions

(*A is Mr. Smith, the manager of Shipment Department in Fast Freight Forwarder, who is speaking with B, Harson from ABC Company.*)

A: Fast Freight Forwarder. May I help you?

B: Yes. This is Harson with ABC Company. You know, we have to avoid Australian customs clearance problems, so our advertising materials and the actual goods to be shipped should be shown on separate packing lists.

A: Oh. I see. Let me take this message.

B: By the way, the ad materials and the goods may be shipped on the same bill of lading.

A: Okay.

B: As some parts of the machines are susceptible to shock, the machines must be packed in seaworthy cases capable of withstanding rough handling.

A: No problem.

B: Thank you for your consideration.

 Warm-up

A. Match the definitions in Column B with the terms in Column A.

A	B
1. load	A. transfer something from one party to another
2. delivery	B. to put a lot of things into a vehicle or machine
3. container	C. a very large metal box used for transporting the goods

Continued

A	B
4. cargo	D. the goods under one contract are shipped in different terms or by different lots
5. partial shipment	E. goods or products transported, generally for commercial gain, by ship or aircraft

B. The following is a passage about the responsibilities of a cargo agent. Fill in the blanks with the words given in the box and discuss with your partners on how to choose the port of loading.

specific   destination   possibility   bear   optional

Port of Loading, which is also called Port of Shipment, is the port where goods are shipped and depart. When determine the port of shipment and port of (1)_____, better be as clear and (2)_____ as possible. Take into account port regulations, facilities, charges and possible sanctions. Be aware of the (3)_____ that different ports may have the same name. Provide some flexibility by allowing (4)_____ ports on the same routes especially when it is hard to make a decision, but do NOT allow too many ports; in such a case specify which party (5)_____ the additional cost that might occur there from.

C. Make up a dialogue according to the following situation.

Student A works as a Customer Service and Transportation Operator in a freight forwarding company, and Student B is an exporter who will export some goods to the USA. Student A and Student B will act out a dialogue about loading.

The dialogue should cover the following information: greetings, the information of the goods to be shipped, the time of shipment and the port of loading.

Section 3   Format Writings and Practical Usages

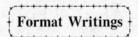

After reading the following passage, you are required to discuss with your partners and to complete the statements that follow the questions.

An Advanced Shipping Notice

An advanced shipping notice or advanced ship notice (ASN) is a notification of pending deliveries, similar to a packing list. It is usually sent in an electronic format and is a common EDI document.

The ASN can be used to list the contents of a shipment of goods as well as additional information relating to the shipment, such as order information, product description, physical characteristics, type of packaging, markings, carrier information, and configuration of goods within the transportation equipment. The ASN enables the sender to describe the contents and configuration of a shipment in various levels of detail and provides an ordered flexibility to convey information.

The ASN is noteworthy in that it is a new concept in logistics, enabled by the advance of modern communication methods. Although it provides information similar to the Bill of Lading, its function is very different. While the Bill of Lading is meant to accompany a load on its path, the goal of the ASN is to provide information to the destination's receiving operations well in advance of delivery. This tends to impact the logistics stream in three areas: cost, accuracy, and flexibility.

Cost. Modern receiving operations rarely have time to break down a shipping unit (carton or pallet) and identify its components, depending instead on quick scans of barcodes on shipping labels. An ASN can provide a list of all of bar coded ID numbers of the shipping units and the contents of each. Receiving costs are thought to be reduced by about 40%.

Accuracy. Upon receipt of the ASN, the receiver is immediately informed of any difference between what was expected, and what has actually been shipped.

Flexibility. Knowing the actual fill rates of the orders gives the receiver the opportunity to re-allocate goods in subsequent shipments.

 ## Problems Solving

1. According to the passage, what is an advanced shipping notice used for?
2. What does "EDI" indicate?
3. According to the passage, what is the function of an ASN?
4. What information can be listed in an ASN?
5. How does an ASN impact the logistics stream?

 ## Writing Samples

Letter 1　Loading Suggestions

April 2, 2024

Dear Sirs,

　　We are pleased to have received your letter of April 1, requiring our suggestions on how to load your product for container shipment.

Please give us the detailed packing size and packages number so that we can advise you on how much of your product can be loaded in a container.

If you do have full container loads, you can arrange to have a container delivered to your warehouse for loading. If you have less than container loads, we suggest you use a consolidator to handle your smaller shipments. Using a consolidator may stretch transit time to 5 to 10 days, but the consolidators are skilled at getting more into less space, so they can help you to reduce your shipping costs.

If you do have a container delivered to your warehouse for stuffing, be sure to turn it around promptly, as there is a charge if you have it "spotted" for more than 48 hours or so. You can arrange service with our trucking line directly. Charges are generally "Per container" form the point of pickup to destination.

And we would think it advisable for you to take advantage of the Roll-on-Roll off for container shipment, this kind of service can offer you considerable savings.

Please note that rail or ocean requires heavier packing than shipment by air, and containerized cargo on ship does not require the same protective packing as cargo going by break bulk.

Yours sincerely,

Letter 2 Shipping Order

April 7, 2024

Dear Sirs,

We are very glad to have received your letter of April 6, 2024, appointing us to be your freight forwarder in China.

Enclosed please find the Shipping Order for the goods to be delivered and we hope you can fill it out and send it back as soon as possible.

We are looking forward to our good cooperation.

Yours sincerely,

Enclosure：

YUN CHANG LOGISTICS（SH）LTD.   SHIPPING ORDER

Shipper (Complete Name and Address)(发货人名称、地址、电话)	Shipper Order No.		
	Export License No.		
Consignee（If to Order State Notify Party）(收货人名称、地址、电话)	上海市运昌国际货运代理有限公司 Yun Chang International Logistics Co., Ltd. 4/F Vicwood Plaza Nanjing Road，Shanghai TEL：+86-021-81457153/81452491 FAX：+86-021-81452472		
Notify Party (通知人)	Freight Status(海运费) ☐ Freight Collect(到付) ☐ Freight Prepaid(预付)	Services Required(服务类型) ☐ CFS/CFS(门/门) ☐ CFS/CY(门/港) ☐ CY/CY(港/港) ☐ CY/CFS(港/门)	
Vessel(船名)	Voyage(航次)		
Port of Loading(起运港)	Port of Origin(港口地)	Number of Original B/L is 3 unless otherwise specify	No. of Container Required(柜型、柜量) 20 ft Box 40 ft Box 40 ft HC
Port of Discharge(目的港)	Final Destination(目的地)		

PARTICULARS DECLARED BY SHIPPER

Marks & Numbers(唛头、包装)	Description of Goods(货物描述)	No. & Kind of Packages(件数)	Gross Weight(kgs)	Measurement(cbm)(体积)
Remarks(备注)		Closing Date/Time(截关日期)		
Container No. (柜号)	Seal No. (封条号)	Warehouse Address(交仓地址)		

IMPORTANT

SHIPPERS ARE REQUESTED TO READ CAREFULLY

Please prepare 5 set copy for warehouse reference.

Shippers are respectfully requested to note that **NO SPECIAL INSTRUCTIONS OR CONDITIONS** can be recognized by the issuer of this Shipping Order unless initialed by the issuer of this Shipping Order.

Carrier reserves the right to reject any package found not in good order and condition.

Neither the Carrier nor its Agents will accept any liability for the consequences of cargo being shut out.

Carriage of cargo is subject to the terms and conditions of the Carrier's Bill of Lading and the applicable tariff.

All transactions are subject to the Company's Standard Trading Conditions （Copies available on request from the Company）and which，in certain cases，exclude or limit the Company's liability.

....
Authorized Signature

Practical Usages

1. Loading Suggestions 装货建议

- If you do have full container loads, you can arrange to have a container delivered to your warehouse for loading.
  如果你方货物够一整箱,你方可以安排将集装箱交仓库装运。
- If you have less than container loads, we suggest you use a consolidator to handle your smaller shipments.
  如果不足一整箱的小批量货物,我们建议你方由集装箱拼箱公司来安排装货。
- If you do have a container delivered to your warehouse for stuffing, be sure to turn it around promptly, as there is a charge if you have it "spotted" for more than 48 hours or so.
  如果你们将集装箱交给仓库装货,一定要尽快装运并抓紧回运。因为置放超过48小时左右的集装箱是要收费的。
- We would think it advisable for you to take advantage of the Roll-on-Roll off for container shipment, this kind of service can offer you considerable savings.
  我们认为你方在进行集装箱运输时,最好使用滚装滚卸,这可以节省一大笔费用。

2. Shipping Order 订舱

- Enclosed please find the Shipping Order for the goods to be delivered.
  随函附寄拟运货物订舱单一份。
- Freight space is difficult to secure on account of heavy congestion.
  由于货运任务拥挤,很难订到舱位。
- The pity is that all the shipping space has been booked up.
  遗憾的是所有舱位都已订出。
- For the balance 75 tons, we have make reservation of freight space on the S. S. Feng Qing.
  关于剩余的75吨货物,我们已订好"丰庆"轮的舱位。

 Problems Solving

1. The following is a letter about shipping advice. Fill in the blanks with the words given below.

| duplicate | inform | execute | assure | covering |

Dear Sirs,

We are now pleased to (1) _____ you that we have shipped the goods under

Contract No. 2458 on board S.S. "Peace" which sails for New York tomorrow.

Enclosed is one set of the shipping documents (2)_____ this consignment, which includes:
- One non-negotiable copy of B/L;
- Commercial invoice in (3)_____;
- One copy of Certificate of Quality;
- One copy of Insurance policy.

We are glad to have been able to (4)_____ your order as contracted and trust that the goods will arrive safely and in good condition.

We take this opportunity to (5)_____ you of our prompt attention in handing your future orders.

Yours sincerely,

2. Discuss with your partners about the procedure in loading the goods.

Section 4 Skills Training and Case Study Samples

Skills Training

A. There are ten incomplete sentences in this part. For each sentence there are three choices marked A, B and C. Choose the one that best completes the sentence.

1. _____ refers to the carriage of the goods from the seller to the buyer, and is realized by transport services.

　　A. Ship　　　　B. Shipment　　　C. Packing

2. In most movement of goods, there are usually three parties: the consignor, the consignee and the _____.

　　A. sellers　　　B. carrier　　　　C. buyers

3. The term Shipping originally referred to transport by _____, but is extended in American English to refer to transport by land or air as well.

　　A. sea　　　　B. bike　　　　　C. train

4. _____ is a note usually sent by the seller to inform the buyer that the goods he has ordered have been dispatched on ship.

　　A. Shipping advice　B. Ship memo　　C. Ship information

5. The chief shipping _____ include Commercial Invoice, Bill of Lading, Insurance Policy or Certificate, Packing List and Weight Memo.

      A. documents   B. information   C. package

6. The basic feature of _____ transport is that at least two modes of transport are used.

      A. cargo   B. ship   C. multimodal

7. _____ freight transport refers to shipments that involve more than one mode.

      A. Air   B. Intermodal   C. Rail

8. FOB is an acronym for "Free on _____", meaning that the seller pays for transportation of the goods. .

      A. Bike   B. Board   C. Bus

9. Bill of Lading is a _____ for goods signed by the shipping company and given to the shippers.

      A. receipt   B. product   C. information

10. The seller should let the buyer know as soon as the shipment is effected, by sending the buyer the shipping _____ together with a set of shipping documents.

      A. information   B. advise   C. advice

B. Translate the following terms into English.

承运人   托运人

收货人   装运通知

海运提单   装船指示

多式联运   装运港

货运单据   运输合同

C. Translate the following sentences into Chinese.

1. Logistics documents contain two kinds of documents: cargo documents and transport documents.

2. B/L is presented at the port of final destination by the importer in order to claim goods.

3. Containers are constructed of metal and are of standards lengths from ten to forty feet.

4. Intermodal transportation offers the opportunity to combine modes and find a less costly alternative than a single transport mode.

5. Since the rate of FCL is relatively low, we suggest you send the goods by FCL.

Case Study Samples

 Sample 1

Transshipment

Transshipment is the shipment of goods or containers to an intermediate destination, then to yet another destination.

One possible reason is to change the means of transport during the journey (for example from ship transport to road transport), known as transloading. Another reason is to combine small shipments into a large shipment (consolidation), dividing the large shipment at the other end (deconsolidation). Transshipment usually takes place in transport hubs. Much international transshipment also takes place in designated customs areas, thus avoiding the need for customs checks or duties, otherwise a major hindrance for efficient transport.

Note that transshipment is generally considered as a legal term. An item handled (from the shipper's point of view) as a single movement is not generally considered transshipped even if it may in reality change from one transport to another at several points. Previously, it was often not distinguished from transloading, since each leg of such a trip was typically handled by a different shipper.

Transshipment is normally fully legitimate and an everyday part of the world's trade. However, it can also be a method used to disguise intent, as is the case with illegal logging, smuggling, or grey market goods.

In a word, transshipment is the act of shipping goods to an intermediate destination prior to reaching their ultimate end-use. Transshipment is a common practice with logistic benefits, but can be used to illegitimately to disguise country of origin or intent of the goods.

 Problems Solving

1. According to the passage, what is transshipment?
2. Suppose you were a seller and you agreed to ship the goods to a buyer on or before December 31 under a CIF Sydney contract. However, you were unable to assemble the goods for delivery in time to reach the ship in Sydney and had to transship the goods by rail to Melbourne, where the ship was taking on goods on

January.

3. Can the buyer refuse to accept the document or to pay the seller? Why?

 Sample 2

K-Mail Shipping Instruction
Loading Requirement

The following forwarders have been assigned to handle merchandise:
- If the goods with different warehouse need to load into one container, supplier must get customer's approval first, and loading sequence must follow up customer's instruction.
- For the air shipment, hanger flat packed garment cannot combine booking with general flat packed garment.
- Utilization of container fill for FCL movement.

The container fill figure detailed below should be followed in order to optimize container fill to minimize freight cost. If supplier cannot meet the target container utilization, approval to ship as FCL must first be sought from customer.

Equipment Type	Minimum Load
20'	17 CBM
40'	38 CBM
40' HQ	62 CBM

-Freight up to 16 CBM should be shipped per LCL

-Freight up to 37 CBM should be shipped per 20' Container (FCL) and Overflow (LCL)

- In the event that there is shortage between the actual load CBM into the container and the CBM advised at time of booking. Supplier will be absorbed the ocean freight difference and extra charges on supplier account.
- Each box must contain only one article number. Mixed boxes of different articles or sizes are not acceptable.
- Do not use any additional outer packaging. Do not bundle article. Do not use any further outer packaging (e.g. foil) or hoops around the box.
- A packing list must always be enclosed with each consignment. On the outside of the shipment/item a viewing envelope with packing list must be attached so

as to be clearly identifiable. A copy should also be attached to the consignment note. If the shipment is not accompanied by a packing list and it cannot be found due to inadequate lettering, this will cost us additional expense, which you will be charged.

 Problems Solving

1. According to the passage, how to ship the freight up to 37 CBM?
2. If there is shortage between the actual load CBM into the container and the CBM advised at time of booking, who will be liable for the ocean freight difference?
3. Suppose you are a freight forwarder. Write a letter to your clients to express your loading requirement.

 ## Section 5 Elevating Vision and Useful Expressions

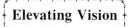

Means of Transportation

There are many means of transportation, and each has its advantages and drawbacks. Goods can be transported by a train, a truck, a plane, a ship or through a pipeline. The method used depends on time and cost.

Trains are usually used to transport bulk products that are low in value and must travel great distances.

Trucks can stop within a city and deliver goods direct to the market. A truck can start as soon as it is loaded. It is mostly used to transport high-value goods which travel short distances.

Air freight is quick although it is expensive. When speed is taken into consideration, this method will be more effective. Food and some urgently needed goods are usually delivered by air freight.

Ships have long been used for transportation. They are still the most important means of transportation in international trade now.

Commodities such as coal, grain, chemicals and iron ore are often shipped by this means. Although it is a little slower, it is much less expensive. So far, most of our export goods have been transported by ship.

Since China began its reform, we have had many busy ports with great handling capacity. Almost 80% of our import and export goods are handled through these ports.

Pipelines are a special form of transportation. This form is being used for transporting gasoline, crude oil, and natural gas. Even some solids can be moved by pipelines.

With the expansion of international trade, the container service has become popular. The use of containers provides a highly efficient form of transport by road, rail and air, which has been regarded as a mode of more efficient shipment.

 Useful Expression

装 货 用 语	
Booking Sheet 订舱单	Liner B/L 班轮提单
Carrier 船公司	M B/L (Master Bill of Lading) 船东提单
Clean B/L 清洁提单	MT B/L (Multimode Transport B/L) 多式联运提单
Consignee 收货人	
CPT (Carriage Paid To) 运费付至目的地	MTD (Multimode Transport Document) 多式联运单据
DAP (Delivered at Place) 目的地交货	
DAT (Delivered at Terminal) 运输终端交货	M/T (Measurement Ton) 尺码吨
DDP (Delivered Duty Paid) 完税后交货	N VOCC (Non Vessel Operating Common Carrier) 无船公共承运人
Direct B/L 直达提单	
Direct Shipment 直航船	Notify Party 通知人
ETA (Estimated Time of Arrival) 预计到达时间	Original B/L 正本提单
ETC (Estimated Time of Closing) 截关日	Place of Delivery 交货地
ETD (Estimated Time of Departure) 预计开船时间	Port of Loading 装货港
FAS (Free Alongside Ship) 装运港船边交货	Received for Shipping B/L 收讫待运提单或待运提单
FCA (Free Carrier) 货交承运人	
FOB (Free on Board) 装运港船上交货	S/O Shipping Order 装货通知书
House Bill of Lading 货运提单	Shipped on Board B/L 已装船提单

Unit 6

Allocation and Transshipment

Learning Objectives

- To know the functions of allocation and transshipment in logistics process
- To learn the key words and expressions of allocation and transshipment

Skill Developing Objectives

- To develop communication skills in dealing with allocation and transshipment
- To develop writing skills in the negotiation of allocation and transshipment

Section 1　　Theme Lead-in

Read the following passage to get a better understanding of this unit.

Transportation

In a board sense, transport or transportation is defined as the movement of people, animals and goods from one location to another. Modes of transport include air, rail, road, water, cable, pipeline and space. The field can be divided into infrastructure, vehicles and operations. Transport is important because it enables trade between persons, which is essential for the development of civilizations.

Transport infrastructure consists of the fixed installations including roads, railways, airways, waterways, canals and pipelines and terminals such as airports, railway stations, bus stations, warehouses, trucking terminals, refueling depots (including fueling docks and fuel stations) and seaports. Terminals may be used both for interchange of passengers and cargo and for maintenance.

Vehicles traveling on these networks may include automobiles, bicycles, buses, trains, trucks, people, helicopters, watercraft, spacecraft and aircraft. Operations deal with the way the vehicles are operated, and the procedures set for this purpose including financing, legalities and policies. In the transport industry, operations and ownership of infrastructure can be either public or private, depending on the country and mode.

Passenger transport may be public, where operators provide scheduled services, or private. Freight transport has become focused on containerization, although bulk transport is used for large volumes of durable items. Transport plays an important part in economic growth and globalization, but most types cause air pollution and use large amounts of land. While it is heavily subsidized by governments, good planning of transport is essential to make traffic flow and restrain urban sprawl.

Transportation moves people and goods from one place to another using a variety of vehicles across different infrastructure systems. It does this using not only technology (namely vehicles, energy, and infrastructure), but also people's time and effort; producing not only the desired outputs of passenger trips and freight shipments, but also adverse outcomes such as air pollution, noise, congestion, crashes, injuries, and fatalities.

Notes

1. In a board sense, transport or transportation is defined as the movement of people, animals and goods from one location to another.

从广义上讲，运输是指把人、动物或货物从一个地方运送至另外一个地方的行为。

2. Transport infrastructure consists of the fixed installations including roads, railways, airways, waterways, canals and pipelines and terminals such as airports, railway stations, bus stations, warehouses, trucking terminals, refueling depots (including fueling docks and fuel stations) and seaports.

交通基础设施是包括公路、铁路、航空、水路、运河、管道及车站等在内的固定设施，如机场、火车站、汽车站、仓库、货运码头、包括燃料码头和燃料站在内的加油站和海港。

3. In the transport industry, operations and ownership of infrastructure can be either public or private, depending on the country and mode.

在运输行业中，车辆的运营和基础设施的所有权可以是公共的，也可以是私人的，这取决于具体的国家和不同的运输模式。

4. Transport plays an important part in economic growth and globalization, but most types cause air pollution and use large amounts of land.

运输在经济增长和全球化的过程中起着极为重要的作用，但是绝大多数的运输模式都对空气造成了污染并占据了大量的土地资源。

Problems Solving

1. What should be considered when we arrange the way of transportation?

2. Decide whether the following statement is true or false.

（1）Transport or transportation is defined as the movement of people, animals and goods from one location to another. （　　）

（2）Vehicles traveling on these networks only include automobiles, bicycles, buses, trains, trucks, people, helicopters and watercraft. （　　）

（3）Freight transport is focused on large volumes of durable items. （　　）

（4）Infrastructure is the traditional preserve of civil engineering. （　　）

（5）Transportation means that moving people and goods from one place to another uses a variety of vehicles across different infrastructure systems. （　　）

Section 2　Conversations and Warm-up

┌ Conversations ┐

 Conversation 1　Transportation Modes

(*A is Tom, a receptionist of a company, who is talking with B, Liu Jiang, a*

client from Hongda Imp. & Exp. Corporation.)

A: Since we have settled the other issues, next let's discuss the mode of transportation of the goods you ordered.

B: All right. Well, I don't think it is proper to transport the goods by railway.

A: How will you ship the order?

B: Air freight is the quickest and safest way, I think.

A: But the freight cost will be higher and that will affect the retail price.

B: Agreed. How about the combined transportation?

A: What's combined transportation?

B: If the goods are to be transshipped from one means of transportation to another during the course of the entire voyage, it's called "combined transportation".

A: What's the advantage of the combined transportation?

B: It's simpler and cheaper to arrange multi-modal combined transportation.

A: I see. From what I've heard you're ready well up in shipping work. About transportation mode, it's up to you.

B: Okay. First. I will check the order to find the quantity and quality about our order. And then, I will compare different transport mode to decide which one is proper for us.

A: All right, if there should be any problem, you can contact me as soon as possible.

B: Okay. I will.

 Conversation 2   Communicating About Shipment

(*A is a staff in Dalian Ocean Shipping Company, who is a carrier and responsible for client service. B is client, who works in Shenyang Chemical Imp. & Exp. Co., Ltd. They are talking inquiry about forwarding business via phone call.*)

A: This is Dalian Ocean Shipping Company. What can I do for you?

B: I am from Shenyang Chemical Imp. & Exp. Co., Ltd. I have 100 MT Bisphenol A (双酚 A) ready for shipment from Rotterdam to Dalian, so I would like to make an enquiry.

A: Thanks for your enquiry. First of all, may I ask some details? When are you going to depart for the shipment?

B: The shipment is not later than April 26, and to be delivered before June 30.

A: There are two voyages for you for your reference. One is the M. V. "Venture

28", which will depart on April 23 and arrive on June 26; the freight rate is USD 1,800 per TEU. The other is the M. V. "Pioneer 8", which is going to leave on April 26 and arrive on June 28, and the freight rate is USD 2,000 per TEU. Addition charges depend on operations of the shipping company, such as inland transport, port handling, and customs formality and so on.

B: I would like to appoint your company for this shipment, including inland transport. And I decide with M. V. "Venture 28".

A: Thank you very much. I will send E-mail to you on the standard form of power of attorney within ten minutes. Please fill in details such as schedule, number of item, type and size of containers, number of containers, gross weight, volume, trade terms and CFS/CFS or CY/CY selection, etc. Please send E-mail back the form with your stamp in an hour.

B: Okay. I will return that in time. Anything else should I send to you?

A: Yes, the following things are required: C/O, trademark license, foreign exchange sales statement, verification form and invoice. We will contact you as soon as possible for materials you are lack of.

B: It's very kind of you.

A: In case of emergency or problems, please contact me as soon as you can. Wish we have a pleasant cooperation!

B: Great! See you later.

 Conversation 3 Arrangement Delivery Cargo

(*This is a conversation by telephone between A and B, both of whom are staff in different companies.*)

A: Morning, Mr. Black. This is Smith. I am calling to inform you that ship carrying your imports reached Tianjin port this morning and has started unloading in the afternoon.

B: Good news for us. Could you tell me when we can expect the goods to arrive at our warehouse?

A: Yes, there are three containers in total. We have to check all the orders of arrangement delivery today. The truck should arrive late Wednesday or early Thursday. It depends on traffic and weather. When will you accept deliveries details?

B: I see. Could you deliver our goods by train?

A: May I ask why? According to our agreement we should deliver them by truck.
B: We hope we can receive the goods as soon as possible. It's faster by train than by truck, isn't it?
A: Don't worry. We'll have no trouble meeting your delivery date. And if a customer requests a carrier other than truck, he must bear the additional charges.
B: Well, in that case, we don't insist on changing the mode of transport if you promise to deliver the goods on time.
A: All right. Thank you.

 Warm-up

A. Match the definitions in Column B with the terms in Column A.

A	B
1. transportation modes	A. the transportation carrier cost to transport goods
2. freight rate	B. different ways or methods about movement of people, animals and goods from one location to another.
3. allocation	C. mode of shipping is used for smaller shipments that are too large to be sent as parcel but too small to fill an entire truckload.
4. less-than-truckload (LTL)	D. the act of distributing by allotting or apportioning
5. voyage charter	E. the practice of hiring or renting cars, buses, planes, etc., for long journey use

B. The following is a passage about packaging. Fill in the blanks with the words given in the box and discuss with your partners about the importance of packaging.

| structure | logistics | economy | transportation | mature |

As China's (1) _____ grows, so grows its transportation and logistics industry. China is becoming a more (2) _____ and self-confident country and a driving force in the new global economic (3) _____, and this is bringing new challenges and opportunities to the five sectors of the country's (4) _____ and (5) _____ industry-express, road freight, air freight, contract logistics and international freight forwarding.

C. Make up a dialogue according to the following situation.

Student A works as a clerk in East Shipping Company, and Student B is a client who is willing to know how to transport the goods to be exported. Student A and Student B will act out the dialogue about transportation modes.

The dialogue should cover the following information: greetings, an introduction to the different transportation modes, and the intention to cooperate.

Section 3 Format Writings and Practical Usages

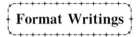

After reading the following passage, you are required to discuss with your partners and to complete the statements that follow the questions.

Air Freight

In recent years air freight has been developing rapidly and air carriers have been able to offer an ever widening range of services. Freight costs can be paid in advance, at destination or against reimbursement.

Advantages of air freight

Air freight has many advantages over other modes of transport. It is generally most practical for goods which have a high unit value. Quick delivery is the most obvious advantage of air freight service, which means a saving of time spent on transit. For this reason, many exporters prefer air freight, especially when they may not be able to afford having their capital tied up for three months while a ship completes her voyage. Furthermore, exporters can benefit from quick delivery of raw materials or finished products, particularly in the export market.

Air freight packing is less expensive than that of consignment by sea. Normally domestic packing is often sufficient; therefore, no extra export packing is required. Lighter packing can be a big advantage in those export transactions for countries where customs duties are based on the total weight of the consignment. Sometimes the saving in this connection is considerable.

The security of air transport is usually superior to that exercised elsewhere, particularly of high value goods. Insurance cost of air transport is usually cheaper than other freight insurance.

Disadvantages of air freight

Air freight has its limitations. There are a number of commodities which are unsuited to be carried by air, including bulky commodities of low value, raw materials, etc., where the high cost of air freight outweighs the other advantages. The gain in speed is sometimes offset by delays due to transfer to ground transport to complete journey, especially so on the shorter journeys. Delays can occur owing to adverse weather conditions. Besides, owing to technical reasons, hazardous cargoes and commodities of awkward sizes are out of the question. Government regulations forbid the transportation of hazardous goods by air.

Problems Solving

1. According to the passage, what are the advantages of air freight?
2. Can you list the disadvantages of air freight?
3. If you are the manager in the company, which mode will you choose among marine cargo transportation, land freight transport and air freight during the purchase of 3,000 computers abroad? Why?

Writing Samples

Letter 1 Urging for Prompt Delivery—End Users Need Goods Urgently

Sept. 16, 2024

Dear Sirs,
Re: Contract No. W4433

  We refer to the above contract signed between us on August 11, 2023 for 6,000 metric tons of wheat, which is stipulated for shipment in March, 2024. However, up till now we have not received from you any information concerning this lot. As our end users are in urgent need of this material, we intend to send our vessel S. S. "Fengqing" to pick up the goods, which is expected to arrive at Ningbo around the end of December. You are requested to let us have your immediate reply by fax or email whether you are agreeable to this proposal. If not, please let us know exactly the earliest time when the goods will be ready.

  We have been put to great inconvenience by the delay in delivery. In case you should fail to effect delivery in December, we will have to lodge a claim against you for the loss and reserve the right to cancel the contract.

Yours faithfully,

Letter 2 Urging for Prompt Delivery—Delivery Time Is Falling Due

May 12, 2024

Dear Sirs,

　　We are very anxious to know about the shipment of our Order No. 123 for 1,000 cases of Tin Plates.

　　As the contracted time of delivery is rapidly due, it is imperative that you inform us of the delivery time without any further delay. We stated explicitly at the beginning the importance of punctual execution of this order and cannot help feeling surprised at your silence about our fax inquiry of April 19, a copy of which is enclosed.

　　We are in urgent need of these goods and have to request you to execute the order within the time stipulated.

Yours faithfully,

Letter 3 Require to Book a Steamer from an Appointed Transportation Company

August 25, 2024

Dear Sirs,

　　Re: Order No. 7767

　　We have received your fax of August 20 and noted that you have booked our Order No. 7767 for four sets of Model 790 Machine. Our confirmation of the order will be forwarded to you in a few days. It is of great importance to our buyers that the arrival date of this order should be arranged as early as possible to meet their requirements. So you are supposed to ship the goods by a steamer of XX Co.. The main reason is that their steamers offer the shortest time for the journey between China and Australia. We shall appreciate it if you try to ship the consignments as follows:

　　Order No. 7767. by S.S. "XX" due to sail from Hamburg on Sept. 18, 2024 or latest by S.S. "XX" due to sail from Hamburg on Sept. 28, 2024 arriving in Shanghai on May 20 and June 3 respectively.

> Thank you in advance for your cooperation.
>
> Yours faithfully,

Practical Usages

1. Negotiation on Transportation 转运谈判

1) To mention the previous contract terms

   提及既定合同条款及安排

- In compliance with the contract stipulations, we forwarded you by air a complete set of non-negotiable documents right after the goods were loaded.

  按合同规定,我们在货物装运后立刻空邮给贵方整套副本单据。

- We wish to advise you that the goods under S/C No. 456 went forward on the steamer "Yunnan" on July 8. They are to be transshipped at Copenhagen and are expected to reach your port in early September.

  兹通知你方,售货合同456号项下的货物已于7月8日装云南轮,经哥本哈根转船,预计9月初可达贵港。

- For the goods under S/C No. 9889, we have booked space on S.S. "East Wind" due to arrive in London around May 20. Please communicate with Lambert Bros Co., London, our shipping agent, for loading arrangement.

  关于售货合同9889号项下的货物,我们已在东风轮上订舱,该轮5月20日左右到达伦敦。请与我船运代理伦敦 Lambert Bros. 公司联系装运事宜。

- We are informed by our supplier that owing to the bad weather your order No. 223 may not be completed in time for shipment by S.S. "East Wind" scheduled to leave here on May 6, 2024.

  从供应商处我们得知,由于气候恶劣,贵方223号订单下的货物可能难以由东风轮及时运达,该轮原定于2024年5月6日驶离此港。

- We are pleased to inform you that your order No. 112 of September 30 has been shipped today per M.V. "Fengqing" which is leaving for Singapore on October 2.

  很高兴告知,贵方9月30日112号订单项下的货物已于今日装风庆轮。该轮定于10月2日驶往新加坡。

- We are pleased to tell you that we have shipped today by S.S. "Red Ring" 100 sets of sewing machines. We believe that the goods will reach you in good order and condition.

很高兴告诉贵方，100台缝纫机已于今日装红环轮。相信该批货会顺利到达贵方且状况良好。

2) To express the expectation for cooperation
   表明合作的意愿

- As we have mentioned in our previous letter, shipment for the suits made to order is not possible in less than three months, but we should like to help you and to give your order special priority.
  如前信所述，虽定做的西服不可能在三个月内发运，我们仍愿帮忙优先考虑贵方订单。
- Transportation plays a very important role in foreign trade.
  运输在国际贸易中起着很重要的作用。
- Which transportation mode should be used depends on time and cost.
  究竟采用哪种运输方式还取决于时间和成本。
- Most import goods have been shipped by sea.
  大部分进口货物都是经由海运的。
- So far there have been over 100 free ports in the world.
  到目前为止，世界上已有一百多个自由港了。
- We shall be pleased to know the time for transit and frequency of sailings, and whether shipping space must be reserved.
  我们想了解一下运输时间、航班次数及是否预留舱位。
- We hope you will arrange early shipment.
  希望你们能早日安排装运。

2. **Avoiding Transportation Errors 避免货运误差**

- Please take the matter up at once and see to it that the goods are delivered without further delay.
  请立即着手交货，务必不可再延误。
- We shall appreciate it if you will effect shipment as soon as possible, thus enabling our buyers to catch the brisk demand at the start of the season.
  如能尽快装运，我们将不胜感激，以便我方买主能赶上销售季节开始时的旺销势头。
- It has to be stressed that shipment must be made within the prescribed time limit, as a further extension will not be considered.
  有必要强调一下，必须在规定的时间内装运，进一步延期将不予考虑。
- A truck can carry goods directly to the market though it can't carry too much at

a time.

虽然卡车一次不能运很多货物，但它可以直接将货物运送到市场上。

- According to the terms of the contract the shipment is to be effected by May 20 and we must have the B/L by May 30 at the latest.

  按照合同条款，应该 5 月 20 日装船。我们必须最迟在 30 日拿到提单。

- As the goods are to be transshipped at Hong Kong, we shall require through B/L.

  因货物需在香港转船，我们要求联运提单。

- As for airway bill, it will be sent to you as soon as the consignment is ready for dispatch by Air China.

  至于空运单，一旦货物备妥待中国航运公司发运，我方立即将其送达贵方。

- We have to advise you that we are unable to dispatch your order in full owing to a great shortage of shipping space.

  我们不得不告知，由于舱位奇缺，我方不能发送所订的全部货物。

Problems Solving

1. Fill in the blanks with the words given below.

| delivery | multimodal | export | afford | expensive |

(1) The carrier responsible for the entire carriage is referred to as a _____ transport operator, or MTO.

(2) Air freight packing is less _____ than that of consignment by sea.

(3) Quick _____ is the most obvious advantage of air freight service, which means a saving of time spent on transit.

(4) Many exporters prefer air freight, especially when they may not be able to _____ having their capital tied up for three months while a ship completes her voyage.

(5) Furthermore, exporters can benefit from quick delivery of raw materials or finished products, particularly in the _____ market.

2. Suppose you are a freight forwarder. Write an e-mail to your client to give some suggestions about transportation. In your e-mail, the following information should be included:

(1) Thanks for his e-mail you received three days ago.

(2) The modes and its rate to be used for the transportation.

(3) To express the expectation for cooperation.

Section 4 Skills Training and Case Study Samples

Skills Training

A. There are ten incomplete sentences in this part. For each sentence there are three choices marked A, B and C. Choose the one that best completes the sentence.

1. _____ is subsequently exchanged for the marine bill of lading.

   A. Booking note   B. Delivery order   C. Dock receipt

2. The booking note is issued by the _____ requesting allocation of shipping space.

   A. carrier to the agent   B. carrier to the shipper
   C. shipper to the carrier

3. The _____ can not be transferred to the third parties by endorsement.

   A. shipped B/L   B. clean B/L   C. straight B/L

4. Time chartering means that the shipowner provides a designated manned ship to the charterer, and the charterer employs the ship for a specific period against payment of hire. Under time chartering, the charterer is not liable for costs such as _____.

   A. bunker costs   B. crew wages   C. port charges

5. Which of the following ports is not within the Far East to Europe and Mediterranean route _____.

   A. Vancouver   B. Antwerp   C. Hamburg

6. Moving goods by rail often involves _____ costs, particularly when the shipper or receiver lacks direct rail access.

   A. transshipment   B. transportation   C. handling

7. Most coal and aggregates are moved in _____ that can be filled and discharged rapidly.

   A. flat wagons   B. refrigerator vans   C. open wagons

8. CIM Rules apply to a contract of carriage by rail, _____.

   A. if the place of taking in charge of goods and the designated place of delivery are situated in two different states, of which at least one is a party to CIM Convention and the parties to the contract agree that the contract is subject to the CIM Rules

   B. if the international carriage includes carriage by road or inland waterway or by sea as a supplement to trans-frontier carriage by rail

C. for all international rail transport

9. _____ provides the basic document for road freight.

    A. A license   B. A bill of lading   C. A road waybill

10. For transport of hazardous materials, truckers have to _____.

    A. affix proper labels for the respective hazard(s) to their vehicle

    B. confirm weight after loading and before delivery

    C. transport in tank trucks or tanker lorries (also road-tankers)

B. Translate the following terms into English.

转运成本　　　　　　货运站

公路运输　　　　　　快速交货

跨境运输　　　　　　欧洲大陆

物权凭证　　　　　　无船承运人

船舶出租人　　　　　托运人

C. Translate the following sentences into Chinese.

1. Characteristics of intermodal transport systems differ across regions.
2. Intermodal transport in the EU will require a comprehensive package of measures both to increase markedly the productivity of rail freight transport and to enforce effective safety, loading, maintenance and working regulations in road haulage.
3. Logistics will influence the future development of intermodal transport, and yield both opportunities and challenges.
4. Since a key factor hindering the wider use of intermodal transport on shorter distances is the substantial share of transshipment costs.
5. National regulations and procedures concerning intermodal transport are not harmonized.

```
Case Study Samples
```

 Sample 1

The Value of Freight

Efficient freight transportation is a very important part of producing products and services and getting them to consumers. Freight transportation services are combined with other logistics inputs such as warehouses, inventories, and information technology in order to provide goods and services to final consumers in a timely fashion.

According to recent information from the U. S. Commodity Flow Survey, on average, 42 tons of freight worth $39,000 was delivered to every person in the United States 15 years ago. When considering the distance involved in transporting this freight, an average of 11,000 ton-miles was delivered to every person in the country. This is equal to carrying almost one ton of freight between the North Pole and the South Pole for every man, woman, and child in the United States or almost two tons between New York and Tokyo for each person.

Quite simply, the system of producing and distributing products to consumers could not exist without the freight transportation network. Freight is hauled by various transportation modes-truck, rail, air, water-and combinations of these modes. The choice of transportation modes or combinations of modes depends on a number of factors including type and value of commodity, distance, and desired speed and reliability of transportation.

For prepackaged food and cosmetics destined for sale after the Expo, the exhibitor or its agent should apply for quality, safety and labeling inspection at entry application. No sale will be permitted without a qualification conclusion. All the food and cosmetics that have been proved unqualified upon inspection will be destroyed or shipped back, or subject to other treatments after the Expo.

 Problems Solving

1. How many values of freight are mentioned in the passage? What are they?
2. How can you support your idea that freight transportation is a very important social part in discussing with others from the value of freight?

 Sample 2

COSCO Caught Out by Bets on Freight Rate

China COSCO Holdings, the world's largest operator of dry-bulk ships in terms of capacity, said that it could lose 3.95bn CNY ($577m) from bad bets on freight rates.

The warning is the latest example of a state-owned Chinese company reporting huge losses from hedging operations.

COSCO blamed "the dramatic change in the recent market" and the drastic drop in freight rates for losses on forward freight agreements, which provide a hedging tool for ship operators.

But analysts said COSCO's positions and subsequent losses were unusually large and could mean the company had beyond hedging by speculating on a rebound in Chinese demand for iron ore, wheat and other commodities shipped by its dry-bulk subsidiaries.

"Nobody in the market was forecasting freight rates would drop so much or so fast," said Cecilia Chan, a transport analyst for Nomura in Hong Kong, "but COSCO's long positions were so big they may have not just been using these contracts to hedge but may also have been speculating as an investment."

The global downturn has caught out a number of large state-owned Chinese companies apparently speculating through their hedging operations to boost earnings.

COSCO said its losses from changes in value of forward freight agreements it held totaled 2.31bn CNY in the first three quarters, but that was offset by gains of 1.87bn CNY on these contracts.

The Baltic Dry Index, which reflects rates on the global dry-bulk shipping market, fell 76% from the end of September to December 12, by which time the company's hedging losses for the year had increased to 5.38bn CNY, offset by just 1.43bn CNY in gains.

The precipitous fall in freight rates was partly caused by a collapse in Chinese demand for iron ore and other commodities as the global economic crisis spread to the world's fastest-growing large economy. A glut of new ships entering the market just as the global crisis hit demand for shipping was also a factor.

Problems Solving

1. Discuss with your classmates how much losses COSCO has suffered from changes in value of forward freight agreements?
2. How to avoid in the future?

Section 5　Elevating Vision and Useful Expressions

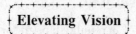

Freight Rate and Its History

Freight rate is about transportation carrier cost to transport goods. Different rates apply for type of goods, distance, weight, size, methods, and directions. A freight rate is a price at which a certain cargo is delivered from one point to another. The price depends on the form of the cargo, the mode of transport (truck, ship, train, and aircraft), the weight of the cargo, and the distance to the delivery destination. Many shipping services, especially air carriers, use dimensional weight for calculating the price, which takes into account both weight and volume of the cargo. For example, bulk coal long-distance rates in America are approximately 1 cent/ton-mile. So a 100 car train, each carrying 100 tons, over a distance of 1,000 miles, would cost $100,000. In ship chartering, freight is the price which a charterer pays a ship-owner for the use of a ship in a voyage charter.

Freight rate, the cost of transporting goods is reflective of a number of factors aside from normal transportation costs. The main determining factors of freight rate are: mode of transportation (truck, ship, train, air craft) weight, size, distance, points of pickup and delivery, and the actual goods being shipped. One of the earliest forms of freight transportation was by water. Many of the earliest settlements were built along or near seacoasts and navigable inland waterways. As these settlements grew, roads and later railroads and pipelines had to be built to transport freight to and from the navigable waterways, thus connecting the inland points of pickup and delivery which could not be reached by navigable waterways.

The development of roads, railroads, and even pipelines allowed for the expansion of settlements inland and away from water ways. Transportation by ships is very limited in nature. If there are no navigable waterways close to the pickup point and destination, then a good will not be transported by a ship. Rarely is any good transported solely by ship, usually goods coming into ports by ship must be unloaded and transferred onto another mode of transportation, i. e. truck or railcar for transportation to its final destination. With the expansion of railroad systems and the development of more efficient trucks, the transportation of freight by ships became less cost effective. Networks, of roads and train tracks which once carried freight from coastal and inland waterway ports to destinations which were not accessible by means of marine transportation, greatly expanded making freight transportation from port to port overland more efficient and more affordable than the marine transportation of freight.

Useful Expression

运 输 用 语	
ABC classification ABC 分类管理	logistics information 物流信息
computer assisted ordering(CAO)计算机辅助订货系统	logistics management 物流管理
	logistics modulus 物流模数
continuous replenishment program（CRP）连续库存补充计划	logistics network 物流网络
	logistics operation 物流作业
customized logistics 定制物流	logistics resource planning（LRP）物流资源计划
distribution logistics 销售物流	
distribution requirements planning（DRP）配送需求计划	logistics strategy 物流战略
	logistics strategy management 物流战略管理
economic order quantity（EOQ）经济订货批量	logistics technology 物流技术
efficient customer response（ECR）有效客户反应	manufacturing resource planning（MRP Ⅱ）制造资源计划
electronic data interchange（EDI）电子数据交换	
electronic order system（EOS）电子订货系统	material requirements planning（MRP）物料需求计划
enterprise resource planning（ERP）企业资源计划	
environmental logistics 绿色物流	military logistics 军事物流
external logistics 社会物流	production logistics 生产物流
fixed-interval system（FIS）定期订货方式	quick response（QR）快速反应
fixed-quantity system（FQS）定量订货方式	returned logistics 回收物流
intangible loss 无形损耗	supply chain 供应链
internal logistics 企业物流	supply chain management（SCM）供应链管理
international logistics 国际物流	supply logistics 供应物流
inventory control 库存控制	tangible loss 有形损耗
just in time（JIT）准时制	third-part logistics（TPL）第三方物流
just-in-time logistics 准时制物流	value-added logistics service 增值物流服务
logistics activity 物流活动	vendor managed inventory（VMI）供应商管理库存
logistics alliance 物流联盟	
logistics center 物流中心	virtual logistics 虚拟物流
logistics cost 物流成本	warehouse layout 仓库布局
logistics cost control 物流成本控制	warehouse management 仓库管理
logistics documents 物流单证	waste material logistics 废弃物物流
logistics enterprise 物流企业	zero-inventory technology 零库存技术

Unit 7

Unloading

Learning Objectives

> To know the procedure of unloading the goods
> To know the responsibilities of relevant parties in unloading the goods
> To learn the key words and expressions in unloading the goods

Skill Developing Objectives

> To develop communication skills in dealing with unloading
> To develop writing skills in dealing with unloading

Section 1   Theme Lead-in

Read the following passage to get a better understanding of this unit.

Unloading

"Unloading" refers to unloading the cargo from the ship at the discharging port, handing over to the consignee or the agent for the consignee at the vessel and transacting the handover procedures. On the one hand, according to the arrival telegram from ship, the agent of the ship-owning company at the discharging port should draw up relevant documents, contact and arrange the berth, get ready for transacting the process of import for the vessel, arrange the stevedoring company and wait for unloading after the arrival of the vessel. On the other hand, the agent of the ship-owning company should inform the consignee the scheduled arrival time of the ship so that the consignee can fully prepare for accepting the goods in time.

Unloading steps

When the goods arrives, at first the computer system will confirm the monthly sailing date arrangement forecast provided by the ship-owning company, arrange the loading machines and berth according to the monthly sailing date arrangement forecast provided by the freight forwarding company, provide the berth arrangement map to the staff of field operation, inform the ship-owning company or the agent the result of the berth arrangement, make the result of berth arrangement a berth alongside schedule and provide it to the customs, immigration control, pilotage or other related units.

Secondly, the control tower of the dock will arrange the locating place for the containers at the storage yard, and inform the storage yard the data of the goods. The staff at the storage yard will determine the tools to be used to unload the goods in the container, arrange the tools and appliance in place, and inform the operation driver and commander to make related preparation and arrange the auxiliary lifting appliance.

After the preparation, the trailer driver should trail the container to the designated spot in the storage yard. The frame crane driver should put the container to a designated spot. The staff in the storage yard and the trailer driver should finish the confirmation for handover.

When the external trailer empty frame for trailing the goods for consignor enters the storage yard, the driver should collect the notepaper with the container locating place information. The driver should trail the container to the designated spot according to the information on the notepaper.

Discharging port

Discharging port, also known as port of destination refers to the last discharging port as the sales contract stipulated. Usually the port of destination is proposed by the buying party and defined after the agreement by the selling party. The port of destination can be one or two or more according to the needs of both parties.

Legal provisions concerning the discharging port

The leaser must unload at the agreed discharging port as the contract stipulates. If there is a term for charterer choosing the unload port, the captain can choose a discharging port agreed in the contract to unload when the charterer failed to inform the determined discharging port timely as the contract stipulates. The charterer must compensate for the loss of the leaser if the charterer doesn't inform the determined discharging port timely as the contract stipulates. The leaser must compensate for the loss of the charterer if the leaser fails to fulfill the contract by choosing the discharging port and unloading arbitrarily and leads the charterer's loss.

 Notes

1. "Unloading" refers to unloading the cargo from the ship at the discharging port, handing over to the consignee or the agent for the consignee at the vessel and transacting the handover procedures.
   卸货是指将船舶所承运的货物在卸货港从船上卸下,并在船舶交给收货人或收货代理人并办理货物交接手续。

2. On the one hand, according to the arrival telegram from ship, the agent of the ship-owning company at the discharging port should draw up relevant documents, contact and arrange the berth, get ready for transacting the process of import for the vessel, arrange the stevedoring company and wait for unloading after the arrival of the vessel.
   船公司在卸货港的代理人根据船舶发来的到港电报,一方面要编制有关单证,联系安排泊位并准备办理船舶进口手续,约定装卸公司,等待船舶进港后卸货。

3. On the other hand, the agent of the ship-owning company should inform the consignee the scheduled arrival time of the ship so that the consignee can fully prepare for accepting the goods in time.
   另一方面还要把船舶预定到港时间通知收货人,以便收货人及时做好接收货物的准备工作。

4. When the goods arrives, at first the computer system will confirm the monthly sailing date arrangement forecast provided by the ship-owning company, arrange the loading machines and berth according to the monthly sailing date arrangement forecast provided by the freight forwarding company, provide the berth arrangement map to the staff of field operation, inform the ship-owning company or the agent the result of the berth arrangement, make the result of berth arrangement a berth alongside schedule and provide it to the customs, immigration control, pilotage or other related units.

   当货物到港时,首先电脑系统会确认船公司向码头提供月度船期安排预报,根据货代公司提供的月度船期安排预报安排装卸机械及泊位,将泊位安排图提供给现场操作人员并将泊位安排结果通知船公司、代理,将泊位安排的结果制成靠泊计划表,提供给海关、边检、引航或其他相关单位。

5. Secondly, the control tower of the dock will arrange the locating place for the containers at the storage yard, and inform the storage yard the data of the goods. The staff at the storage yard will determine the tools to be used to unload the goods in the container, arrange the tools and appliance in place, and inform the operation driver and commander to make related preparation and arrange the auxiliary lifting appliance.

   其次,码头控制塔安排集装箱在堆场的摆放位置,并将货物资料通知堆场。堆场人员确定装卸集装箱要使用的工具,并安排工具及器械到位,堆场人员通知操作司机及指挥人员做相关准备,并安排辅助吊具。

6. After the preparation, the trailer driver should trail the container to the designated spot in the storage yard. The frame crane driver should put the container to a designated spot. The staff in the storage yard and the trailer driver should finish the confirmation for handover.

   经过准备工作,拖车司机按照指令将集装箱拖至堆场指定位置。龙门吊司机将集装箱摆放到指定位置,堆场人员与拖车司机完成工作交接确认。

7. When the external trailer empty frame for trailing the goods for consignor to enter into the storage yard, the driver should collect the notepaper with the container locating place information.

   当为货主拖运货物的外部拖车空架进入码头堆场时,司机应当领取记录有集装箱摆放位置信息的便条纸。

8. Discharging port, also known as port of destination refers to the last discharging port as the sales contract stipulated.

卸货港,又称目的港,是指买卖合同规定的最后卸货港口。

9. Usually the port of destination is proposed by the buying party and defined after the agreement by the selling party.

    目的港一般由买方提出,经卖方同意后确定。

10. The leaser must unload at the agreed discharging port as the contract stipulates.

    出租人应当在合同约定的卸货港卸货。

11. If there is a term for charterer choosing the unload port, the captain can choose a discharging port agreed in the contract to unload when the charterer failed to inform the determined discharging port timely as the contract stipulates.

    合同订有承租人选择卸货港条款的,在承租人未按合同约定及时通知确定的卸货港时,船长可以从约定的选卸港中自行选定一港口卸货。

12. The charterer must compensate for the loss of the leaser if the charterer doesn't inform the determined discharging port timely as the contract stipulates.

    承租人未按照合同约定及时通知确定的卸货港,致使出租人遭受损失的,应当承担赔偿责任。

13. The leaser must compensate for the loss of the charterer if the leaser fails to fulfill the contract by choosing the discharging port and unloading arbitrarily and leads the charterer's loss.

    出租人未按照合同约定,擅自选定港口卸货致使承租人遭受损失的,应当承担赔偿责任。

 Problems Solving

1. Fill in the blanks with the words given below.

| confirm | storage | stipulated | compensate |
| designated | berth | discharging | proposed |

(1) The agent of the ship-owning company at the discharging port should arrange the _____ according to the arrival telegram from ship.

(2) The computer system will _____ the monthly sailing date arrangement forecast provided by the ship-owning company.

(3) The control tower of the dock will arrange the locating place for the containers at the _____ yard.

(4) Discharging port refers to the last discharging port as the sales contract _____.

(5) The leaser must _____ for the loss of the charterer if the leaser fails to fulfill the contract.

(6) Unloading refers to unloading the cargo from the ship at the _____ port.

(7) Usually the port of destination is _____ by the buying party and defined after the agreement by the selling party.

(8) The trailer driver should trail the container to the _____ spot in the storage yard.

2. Discuss with your partners about unloading procedure in freight services.

Section 2　Conversations and Warm-up

 Conversations

Conversation 1　Determining Port of Unloading

(*A is Mr. Wang, the sales manager of Wanda Company, who is speaking with B, a clerk in a freight forwarding company.*)

A: How long does it usually take for you to make delivery?

B: Delivery would be a month from receipt of your order.

A: Could you effect shipment more promptly?

B: I'm sorry to say that we can't advance the time of delivery. Getting the goods ready, making out the documents and booking the shipping space, all these take time.

A: I see. Where is your unloading port?

B: There are more sailings at Port Elisabeth, so we have chosen it as the unloading port.

A: We'd like to change the unloading port to Capetown.

B: No problem. It makes no difference to us to change the unloading port from Port Elisabeth to Capetown.

A: That'll be fine. I appreciate your cooperation.

Conversation 2　Changing Port of Destination

(*A is Johnson with Swift Forwarder Company, who is speaking with B, Mr. Smith from Miller Company.*)

A: Swift Forwarder. What can I do for you?

B: This is Jim Smith from Miller Company. I'd like to know whether you can change the port of destination of our cargo.

A: What cargo?

B: The dresses to Toulouse. I remember the consignment consists of twenty TEU.

A: Let me see. The ship that carries your containers is still at Suez, waiting for the transit of the Suez Canal. It will not pass the canal in 48 hours. We can send a cable to the ship and the port of Marseilles and tell them.

B: Thank you very much.

A: You are welcome. But I must have the three original Bills of Lading.

B: Oh, they are now on their way to the consignee. Why do you want them?

A: We would like to make sure that no third party will claim the cargo with any of the original B/L.

B: Do you accept Letter of Indemnity?

A: We have to make a commercial decision and take the risk ourselves. But considering you are our long time customer, we accept it.

B: Thank you. I will send you a Letter of Indemnity and contact the customer and ask them to pay for the extra expense that may incur when the containers are moved.

 Conversation 3   Wrong Delivery

(*A, an importer, has received the wrong delivery and is making a complaint to B, a freight forwarder.*)

A: Upon the examination of your delivery, we find it does not contain the goods we imported. No doubt, you have made an error.

B: Would you please tell us in detail?

A: We imported tablecloths, whereas the contents are towels. Evidently, the goods are wrong. We are holding the goods for your disposal in our warehouse.

B: The mistake is entirely on our side. We'll try to bring the case to a speedy close and arrange to send you replacement immediately.

A: That's great.

B: Sorry for the inconvenient caused. We are prepared to allow 15% off the freight charges for the losses we have made to you.

A: Thank you for your consideration.

Warm-up

A. Match the definitions in Column B with the terms in Column A.

A	B
1. unload	A. the place where someone is going or where something is being sent or taken
2. consignee	B. the person to whom merchandise is delivered over
3. dock	C. a part of a port where ships are repaired, or where goods are put onto or taken off them
4. destination	D. notice of readiness
5. N. O. R	E. to remove the contents of something, especially a load of good from a vehicle

B. The following is an introduction to a port. Fill in the blanks with the words given in the box and then discuss with your partners about the function of a port.

traffic   shelter   location   ship   harbor

A port is a (1) _____ on a coast or shore containing one or more (2) _____ where ships can dock and transfer people or cargo to or from land. Port locations are selected to optimize access to land and navigable water, for commercial demand, and for (3) _____ from wind and waves. Ports with deeper water are rarer, but can handle larger, more economical (4) _____. Since ports throughout history handled every kind of (5) _____, support and storage facilities vary widely, may extend for miles, and dominate the local economy. Some ports have an important military role.

C. Make up a dialogue according to the following situation.

Student A works as a transportation operator in a freight forwarding company, and Student B is an importer who will import some goods from Australia. Student A and Student B will act out the dialogue about unloading.

The dialogue should cover the following information: greeting, an introduction to the port of unloading, and the change to the port of destination.

 ## Section 3 Format Writings and Practical Usages

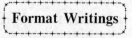

After reading the following passage, you are required to discuss with your partners and to complete the statements that follow the questions.

Port of Delivery and Port of Discharge

This is one of the common doubts among traders, the difference between port of delivery and port of discharge. Is there any difference between port of discharge and place of delivery? The port of discharge and place of delivery is commonly mentioned in the bill of lading. The term Port of Discharge means, the Port in which the goods are discharged. However, if the port of delivery has been mentioned in the bill of lading, the responsibility to deliver goods at place mentioned in Bill of Lading is vested with the carrier of goods.

Port of discharge can be a destination sea port, where in Place of delivery be at an inland location away from port of discharge. If the carrier accepted goods from shipper to deliver at a port other than port of discharge, the cost of delivering cargo from port of discharges to the place mentioned to deliver cargo has to be met by the carrier of goods.

If the carrier accepts goods up to port of discharge only, the column "place of delivery" or "port of delivery" leave blank, which means the liability of carrier to deliver cargo is only up to port of discharge.

 Problems Solving

1. According to the passage, what is one of the common doubts among traders?
2. In which document is the port of discharge and place of delivery commonly mentioned?
3. According to the passage, is the port of discharge same as a destination sea port?
4. What does it mean if the carrier accepts goods up to port of discharge only and the column "place of delivery" or "port of delivery" leave blank?
5. Do you think the port of discharge and place of delivery are the same? Why?

 Writing Samples

Letter 1　Notice of Readiness

April 3, 2024

Dear Sirs,

　　This is to notify that the shipment of 10,000 foot wears has arrived at Capetown port No. 3 anchorage at 12:30 hours on April 3, 2024 and the port entering formalities for M/V Peace were passed at 16:00 hours April 3, 2024.

Now she is ready in all respects to commence loading her cargoes in according with the terms and conditions of the charter party.

The master of M/V Peace has tendered this notice of readiness at 1245 hours on April 3, 2024.

The agent from PENAVICO Shanghai has received notice of readiness at 19:00 hours on April 3, 2024.

Yours sincerely,

Letter 2　Unloading Requirements

April 11, 2024

Dear Sirs,

Please send us the Bill of Lading, stowage plan for our coordination to the consignees.

At the mean time, we breakdown hereunder the expenses for M/V Peace, as per our e-mail yesterday:

Stevedoring cost for 15,000M/T liner out cargo, including vessel operation—$4,500

Estimated port disbursement plus agency fee—$7,200

Tallying charges on vessel side at $0.2per M/T

(15,000×$0.2=3,000)

Grand Total: $14,700

We would appreciate if you could instruct master to send us his firm ETA Shanghai.

Thank you for your cooperation.

Yours faithfully,

Practical Usages

1. Notice of Readiness 装/卸备妥通知书

- This is to notify that the shipment of 10,000 foot wears has arrived at Capetown port No. 3 anchorages at 12:30 hours on April 3, 2024, and the port entering formalities for M/V Peace were passed at 16:00 hours April 3, 2024.

兹通知你方10000件鞋类产品已于2024年4月3日12:30时抵达开普敦港口3号泊位。船舶于2024年4月3日16:00时完成入港手续。

- Now she is ready in all respects to commence loading her cargoes in according with the terms and conditions of the charter party.

  按照租船规定,现已准备开始卸货。

- I have the pleasure to inform you that the Joanna arrived here safely yesterday, just in time to get them discharged before holidays commence.

  我很高兴地通知您,昨天"乔安娜号"安全到达这里,正好赶在假期开始之前卸货。

- This is to advise you that Hope arrived at Tianjin at 12:45 hours on March 25, 2024.

  兹通知您,"希望"号到达天津的时间是2024年3月25日的12点45分。

- I am writing to inform you that your goods will be unloaded in an hour.

  我写信通知您,您的货物将在一个小时内被卸载。

2. Unloading Requirements 卸货要求

- Please send us the Bill of Lading, stowage plan for our coordination to the consignees.

  请寄送提单和积载图,以便我方与收货人接洽。

- Stevedoring cost for 15,000M/T liner out cargo, including vessel operation—$4,500.

  装卸15,000公吨货物的费用,承运人付卸货费,包括船舶移泊费共计4,500美元。

- We would appreciate if you could instruct master to send us his firm ETA Shanghai.

  如指示你方船长把抵达上海港的准确时间告知我方,我们将不胜感激。

- Further to your e-mail this morning, please advise vessel's latest discharge position and ETCD.

  再次回复你方今晨的电子邮件,请告知船舶最新卸货动态和完货时间。

 Problems Solving

1. What is NOR? Could you give an example of NOR?
2. The following is a passage about unloading the goods. Fill in the blanks with the words given below.

notify	master	formalities	anchorage	slip

We have received the _____ from your bank, for which we thank you very much. Yesterday we also received the cable from the _____ of M/V East Star, which is to _____ that the goods have arrived at London port No. 2 _____ at 15:30 hours on April 12, 2024 and the port entering _____ for M/V East Star were passed at 19:00 hours April 12, 2024.

Section 4　Skills Training and Case Study Samples

Skills Training

A. There are ten incomplete sentences in this part. For each sentence there are three choices marked A, B and C. Choose the one that best completes the sentence.

1. A port is a _____ on a coast or shore containing one or more harbors where ships can dock and transfer people or cargo to or from land.

　　A. ship　　　　　　B. location　　　　　C. locate

2. This is one of the common doubts among traders, the difference between port of delivery and port of _____.

　　A. discharge　　　　B. carrier　　　　　C. buying

3. Port of discharge can be a destination _____ port.

　　A. sea　　　　　　B. dock　　　　　　C. train

4. If the carrier accepts goods up to port of discharge only, the column "place of delivery" or "port of delivery" leave blank, which means the _____ of carrier to deliver cargo is only up to port of discharge.

　　A. liability　　　　 B. memo　　　　　 C. information

5. _____ refers to unloading the cargo from the ship at the discharging port, handing over to the consignee or the agent for the consignee at the vessel and transacting the handover procedures.

　　A. Documents　　　 B. Unloading　　　　C. Load

6. When the goods arrives, at first the computer system will _____ the monthly sailing date arrangement forecast provided by the ship-owning company.

　　A. inform　　　　　B. confirm　　　　　C. copy

7. Discharging port, also known as port of _____ refers to the last discharging port as the sales contract stipulated.

　　A. place　　　　　　B. destination　　　　C. rail

8. The agent of the ship-owning company should inform the consignee the scheduled _____ of the ship so that the consignee can fully prepare for accepting the

goods in time.

A. arrival time   B. departure time   C. leaving time

9. Usually the port of destination is proposed by the _____ party and defined after the agreement by the selling party.

A. selling   B. buying   C. producers

10. The leaser must unload at the _____ discharging port as the contract stipulates.

A. agreed   B. advised   C. advice

B. Translate the following terms into English.

目的港   卸货港
承租人   出租人
泊位   延迟交货
船期   离港时间
码头   装卸备妥通知书

C. Translate the following sentences into Chinese.

1. We are always willing to choose the big ports as the unloading ports.
2. It makes no difference to us whether the unloading port is Shantou or Zhuhai.
3. We'll designate Washington as the unloading port, for it is close to our customers.
4. We do hope you will contact the shipping company once again to make sure that the shipment will arrive in Hamburg.
5. I have the pleasure to inform you that the Joanna arrived here safely yesterday, just in time to get them discharged before holidays commence.

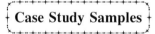

Case Study Samples

Sample 1

Port of Delivery

For the standard trade terms (FOB, FAS, CIF, CFR) which only apply to marine transport, inland cities cannot be their port of discharge. For example, when trade with the inland areas; inland cities cannot be used as the port of discharge. You can arrange shipping ports which is close to the city as the port of discharge unless you switch to other trade terms. Discharging port only indicates the port where the goods are unloading from the ship. If the discharging port and the destination port are the same one, only one will be displayed. If the discharging port and the destination port are not the same one, the names and the addresses of discharging port and the destination port should be listed clearly.

Port of delivery is decided by your way of closing the deal. The ports of delivery for CIF and FOB are different. For example, for FOB Shanghai is the port of delivery while for CIF Busan is the port of delivery. The discharging port as to the cargo, there are many discharging port on the way to the destination port. The destination port as to the ship, the destination port refers to the ship's final destination. The two can combine as one at the final port of destination.

Determination on the loading port and discharging port listed in the ocean bill of lading is not only an important issue which the import and export trading companies often encounter when they deal with the ocean bill of lading but also a major project when the bank audit the bill of lading in the letter of credit operation.

Reflecting this issue on the letter of credit settlement business can be summarized as: How to understand the provision for loading port and discharging port in the letter of credit correctly, and accurately fill in relevant transportation column accurately in the bill of lading. There are specific provisions to the loading port and discharging port in the letter of credit. In today's letter of credit operation, SWIFT and TELEX are two common ways. According to explanation by SWIFT organization, domain 44A (loading in charge) in the letter of credit which adopts MKT700 standardized format usually indicates the locations for shipment, delivery and accepting supervision while domain 44B (for transportation to) indicates the destination for delivery of goods. In the format of TELEX, the issuing bank often use "from... to..." to stipulate the routes of freightage and ports concerned. Accordingly, place of receipt, loading port and port of discharge are usually printed in the format of bill of lading.

Problems Solving

1. What is discharging port?
2. What is destination port?
3. What is the difference between destination port and port of delivery?

Sample 2

Laytime

In commercial shipping, laytime is the amount of time allowed (in hours or days) in a voyage charter for the loading and unloading of cargo. If the laytime is exceeded, demurrage is incurred. If the whole period of laytime is not needed, dispatch may be payable by the ship-owner to the charterer, depending on the terms of the charter party (dispatch does not apply to tanker charters).

Laytime and laydays are often confused as referring to the same idea. Laydays refers to the time when a ship must present it to the charterer. If the ship arrives before the laydays specified, the charterer does not have to take control or start loading (depending on the type of charter). If the ship arrives after the laydays, then the contract can be cancelled—hence laydays are often presented as the term Laydays and Cancelling and can be shortened to Laycan.

The point when laytime commences is determined by a Notice of Readiness (NOR), which the master or agent of the ship must give to the charterer when the ship has arrived at the port of loading or discharge. The NOR informs the charterer that the ship has arrived at the port and is ready in all respects to load or discharge.

Problems Solving

1. What is laydays? Why is the term Laydays often shortened to Laycan?
2. What is NOR? Try to make a NOR to the buyer to state the unloading situation.

Section 5　Elevating Vision and Useful Expressions

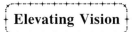

Fixture Note

租船合同

Contract No: HD23lc

Date: Jan. 1, 2024

It is mutually agreed and confirmed by and between MAR UN LTE as owner and COSCO as charterers on the following terms and conditions:

1. Performing vessel (船名): MV. LE HE OR SUB TBN
2. Cargo & Quantity (货物及数量): Abt 8.31 CBM /78.69 MT of equipments, as part cargo Owner's deck option.

3. Load/Discharge Port（装/卸港）：1 sbp Shanghai, China / 1 sbp Jubail, Saudi Arabia.

4. Laycan（受载期/消约期）：11-17 /Mar., 2024

5. Freight rate（运费）：USD in lump sum W/M on FLT terms including L/S/D charge basis 1/1

6. Detention charge（滞期费）：Charterer shall pay Owner 22,000USD pdpro if cargos or/and cargos documents not ready before vessel arrival at loading/discharging port, and if receivers do not take cargo fast as vessel can deliver. Detentions, if any, to be settled between Charterer and Owner within five days of presentation of all relevant documents bends, but always before discharging complete.

7. Laydays（装卸时间）：Shall commence once notice of readiness

8. Documentation fee（文件费）：350.00 CNY per B/L

9. Load/Discharge rate（装/卸率）：5000/1500 PDPR SSHEXUU

10. Deck/Under deck（装甲板/装货舱内）：Owner's option

11. Freight Payment（海运费）：Full freight payable to owner's nominated bank account free of any bank charges levied by remitters bank and/or their correspondence bank to owners w/i three banking days acol. Freight Prepaid B/L to be s/r only upon full freight received. Freight deemed earned upon completion of loading, discount-less and non-returnable whether ship and/or cargo lost or not lost.

12. Wharfages/Taxes/Dues（码头费/税费/应付账款）：On cargo to be for Charterer's account, same on vessel/freight to be for Owner's account.

13. Tally（理货费）：Shipside tally to be for Owner's account, shoreside tally to be for charter's account.

14. Arbitration（仲裁）：If any, in Hong Kong and English law to apply and the arbitration award shall be final and binding on the parties.

15. Owners agent at bends. 装卸港均由船东安排代理。

16. Cargo delivery/receiving（提货/收货）：At the load port or discharge port, if it's mandatory due to port regulations for the cargo to be delivered or received directly under hook by trucks, rail wagons or lighter, charterer to ensure the cargo be delivered or received as fast as the ship is able to load or discharge respectively, otherwise demurrage/detention to apply. Subsequent loss of charter due to the detention is on charterer's account.

17. General average to be settled as per York-Antwerp Rules 197

18. Others as per GENCON c/p 94.

For and on behalf of owners: XXXX   For and on behalf of charterer: XXXX

 Useful Expression

卸 货 用 语	
clearance B/L 运费后付提单	installment shipment 分批装船
combined transport bill of lading 联合货运提单	interior transportation 国内运输
conference rates 公会费率	international railway through transport 国际铁路联运
consignee 收货人	
consigner 发货人	land transportation 陆运
delayed shipment 装船延期	lay days 装卸时间
delivered weight 卸货时的重量	letter of indemnity 赔偿保证书
delivery ex-warehouse 仓库交货	notice of readiness 装/卸备妥通知书
delivery order 提货单	order bill of lading 指示提单
delivery point 交货地点	part of space 部分舱位
destination port 目的港	partial shipment 分批装船
deviation from voyage route 改变航线	shipping document 货运单据
discharge of goods 卸货	shipping notice 装运通知
dock receipt 收货单	short delivery 短交
documents against payment 付款交单	shipping space 载位
full container load 集装箱整装或整交	short shipment 装载不足
gross landed weight hatch 卸货毛重	spot delivery 现场交货
hatch 船舱	

Unit 8

Documentation

Learning Objectives

- To know the functions of different documents
- To make out the documents required in freight services
- To know the requirements of various documents

Skill Developing Objectives

- To develop communication skills in preparing the documents
- To develop writing skills in preparing the documents

Section 1　Theme Lead-in

Read the following passage to get a better understanding of this unit.

Documents in Foreign Trade

One of the major differences between domestic trade and foreign trade is documentation. Every shipment must be accompanied by a number of correct documents. If they are not the correct ones, the importer will have difficulties in taking delivery of the goods, and delays caused by incorrect documentation may affect future business relations between the trading partners.

Different documents are required for different transactions, depending on the nature of the deal, the term of delivery, the type of commodity, stipulations of credit, regulations and practices in different countries, etc. However, most transactions require the following major documents:

Commercial Invoice

This document is the general description of the quality and quantity of the goods and the unit and total price. It constitutes the basis on which other documents are to be prepared. It should be noted that the description of the goods in the invoice must comply with the credit and that the total invoice value should not exceed the total amount of the covering L/C.

Packing List

It gives information such as the number, date, name and description of the goods, shipping marks, packing, number of packages, specific contents of each package and its net weight and gross weight, etc. Sometimes the credit stipulates for specification list which is similar to the packing list but emphasizes the description of the specifications of the goods.

Weight List

It is similar to the packing list in content and function but put emphasis on the weight of the goods and is generally used for goods which are based on the weight for price calculation.

Bill of Lading

It is one of the most important documents and serves as a cargo receipt signed by the carrier and issued to the shipper or consignor. It constitutes a contract of carriage and is a document of title to the goods.

There are quite a few types of bills of lading classified in several ways. However, most letters of credit stipulate for "clean, on board bill of lading". A clean bill of lading is one which states that the goods have been shipped in apparent good order and condition. An on board bill of lading indicates that the shipment has been actually loaded on the carrying vessel bound for the port of destination.

Waybill

The document similar to the ocean bill of lading is called airway bill for air transportation and railway bill, cargo receipt, etc. for railway transportation.

Insurance Documents

The insurance policy and the insurance certificate are similar in function, the only difference being that the latter is a bit simpler than the former.

Certificates

Various certificates may be required depending on the nature of the commodity and the stipulations of the specific countries. The major types are certificate of quality, certificate of weight, certificate of quantity, certificate of disinfection, veterinary certificate, certificate of origin, etc.

Other documents that may be required are customs invoice, consular invoice, consular visa, shipping advice, etc.

 Notes

1. Different documents are required for different transactions, depending on the nature of the deal, the term of delivery, the type of commodity, stipulations of credit, regulations and practices in different countries, etc.
   根据交易性质、交货方式、商品类型、信用证规定,以及各国规章制度与惯例,交易不同,所需的单据也不尽相同。
2. It should be noted that the description of the goods in the invoice must comply with the credit and that the total invoice value should not exceed the total amount of the covering L/C.
   需要注意的是,发票中有关货物的描述必须与信用证相符,发票金额不应超过信用证金额。
3. Sometimes the credit stipulates for specification list which is similar to the packing list but emphasizes the description of the specifications of the goods.
   有时信用证规定的货物规格与装箱单有些相似,但信用证更强调货物规格的具体描述。
4. A clean bill of lading is one which states that the goods have been shipped in apparent good order and condition.

清洁提单表明了货物在装运时表面状况良好。

5. The insurance policy and the insurance certificate are similar in function, the only difference being that the latter is a bit simpler than the former.
保单与保险凭证有着相似的功能,唯一的区别在于后者在形式上比前者简单。

6. Various certificates may be required depending on the nature of the commodity and the stipulations of the specific countries.
根据货物性质以及各国的具体规定,外贸中可能需要各式各样的证明文件。

Problems Solving

1. There are quite a few types of bills of lading classified in several ways. Can you list them all?

2. Decide whether the following statement is true or false according to the passage?

(1) The insurance policy and the insurance certificate are quiet different in form and in function.   (   )

(2) The total invoice value can exceed the total amount of the covering L/C.
   (   )

(3) A Bill of lading is a document of title to the goods.   (   )

(4) Most letters of credit stipulate for clean, on board bill of lading.   (   )

(5) Packing list is the basis on which other documents are to be prepared.   (   )

Section 2 Conversations and Warm-up

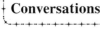

Conversation 1   Variety of Documents

(A is Ms. Li, the manager of a shipping company, who is talking with B, Mr. Wang, a documentary clerk.)

A: Hello, Mr. Wang. It seems that you are worried about something.

B: Well, I'm puzzled about the variety of documents in freight forwarding.

A: Yes, there are a lot of documents, which belong to five scopes: financial documents, commercial documents, shipping documents, insurance documents and other documents.

B: So many!

A: Financial documents include Bill of Exchange, Check, and L/C; commercial documents refer to Commercial Invoice and Packing List; shipping documents include Booking Note, Shipping Order, Mate's Receipt, Bill of Lading, Multimode Transport Document, Air Waybill, Shipping Advice, Delivery Order, and so on.

B: How about insurance documents?

A: They are some documents related with insurance like Insurance Policy. There are other documents that play important roles in doing business.

B: What are they?

A: For example, Import or Export License, Certificate of Origin, Certificate of Quality and others.

B: Thank you for your introduction.

 Conversation 2   Requirements of Documents Production

(*A is Zhang Hua, a college student, who is talking with B, Mr. Smith, a clerk with a freight forwarding company.*)

A: As you have rich experience in documents production, could you tell me what I should pay attention to while making out documents?

B: Of course. According to my experience, there are five requirements. They are correctness, completeness, punctuality, conciseness and tidiness.

A: Could you explain them?

B: Correctness is the premise of making documents successfully. Any documents should obey laws and comply with industry rules such as the International Trade Practice.

A: I think the documents should be made in accordance with details of goods.

B: That's right. The requirement of completeness refers to three aspects: Content should be complete; types should be complete; and copies should be complete.

A: I see.

B: The third requirement is punctuality. The process of making out documents is complicated, which needs cooperation from other units or parties. So anyone involved should set to work in time.

A: I've learned that only necessary information could be presented in documents. Am I right?

B: Yes, it is true. According to the rules, in order to prevent confusion and misunderstanding, banks should discourage excessive filling in or any amendment to details of content.

A: OK. Then I guess tidiness means that documents should be clear, clean, beautiful, and the format should be designed reasonably.

B: Yes, you are right.

 Conversation 3　Types of Bill of Lading

(*A is Johnson, a new comer, who is talking with B, Daniel, a clerk with rich experience in freight forwarding services.*)

A: Could you introduce the types of B/L to me?

B: Of course. You know B/L is a kind of document needed in collection with the bank. And it plays an important role in contacting carrier in the transport of goods, providing proof of transport cost, and making claims.

A: So we must know its type and function.

B: According to the rules, the seller must provide on board bill of lading, which is always issued after shipment.

A: That's the reason why it's called "on board bill of lading".

B: Yes. In international trade settlement, the bank will only accept clean B/L.

A: What does that mean?

B: That means the carrier did not mark the condition of goods as adverse situation. Or the surface of the cargo is in good condition while receiving it.

A: I got it. Then what is sea waybill?

B: Sea waybill is used more frequently than before. It does not confer title of the goods to the bearer, and as a result there is no need for the physical document to be presented for the goods to be released.

A: Anything else?

A: Yes. Straight B/L can not be transferred to others, while bearer B/L is a kind of negotiable document. Such B/L does not specify a consignee, so the delivery shall be made to whoever holds the bill.

B: I got them. That means I should pay special attention to them while dealing with documents. Thank you!

 Warm-up

A. Match the definitions in Column B with the terms in Column A.

A	B
1. bill of lading	A. a written contract between a person and an insurance company
2. insurance policy	B. a document issued by a carrier which details a shipment of merchandise and gives title of that shipment to a specified party

Continued

A	B
3. commercial invoice	C. a document issued by authorities to allow an activity that would otherwise be forbidden
4. certificate of origin	D. a document certifying that the goods have been wholly produced in a particular country
5. license	E. a document issued by a seller, indicating specific information such as the name of commodity, quantities, and agreed price

B. The following is a passage about B/L. Fill in the blanks with the words given in the box and then discuss with your partners about the types of Bills of Lading.

merchandise   prior   endorsed   carrier   documents

Bills of Lading are one of three important (1) _____ used in international trade to help guarantee that exporters receive payment and importers receive (2) _____. A straight bill of lading is used when payment has been made in advance of shipment and requires a (3) _____ to deliver the merchandise to the appropriate party. An order bill of lading is used when shipping merchandise (4) _____ to payment, requiring a carrier to deliver the merchandise to the importer, and at the endorsement of the exporter the carrier may transfer title to the importer. (5) _____ order bills of lading can be traded as a security or serve as collateral against debt obligations.

C. Make up a dialogue according to the following situation.

Student A works as a documentary clerk in a freight forwarding company, and Student B is a new comer. Student A and Student B will act out the dialogue about preparing freight forwarding documents.

The dialogue should cover the following information: the kinds of logistics documents, the types of B/L, and the requirements in documents production.

Section 3   Format Writings and Practical Usages

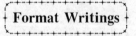

After reading the following passage, you are required to discuss with your partners and to complete the statements that follow the questions.

Bill of Lading

The bill of lading (abbreviated as B/L) is issued to the exporter by the carrier transporting the merchandise. It has a variety of purposes in international trade aside from the main purpose of providing a record of shipment for goods.

It is a receipt for the goods. As a receipt, the bill of lading notes that the carrier has received the goods described on the face of document.

It is a document of title. The bill of lading confers title to the goods to the consignee noted on the bill. The bill of lading may also be made out "To Order", which confers title to the goods to the holder of the bill of lading.

It is the evidence of the contract of carriage. The bill of lading specifies that the carrier is obligated to provide a transportation service in return for a certain charge. Under the B/L, both carrier and consignee have separate rights and obligations. If different opinions arise, it is the law base for them to resolve disputes.

Besides, it is a negotiable instrument. Because the bill of lading represents title to the goods detailed upon it, it can be traded in much the same way as the goods may be, and even borrowed upon if desired. This is a very important and common document used in export and import trade globally.

Problems Solving

1. What is the Bill of Lading?
2. How many purposes does the Bill of Lading serve? What are they?
3. How many types of Bill of Lading do you know? List them all.
4. If disputes arise, why should we call the Bill of Lading as the law base?
5. We say that the Bill of Lading can be borrowed or traded like goods. Why?

Writing Samples

Letter 1 Sending Documents

May 10, 2024

Dear Sir,

We are pleased to acknowledge receipt of your letter of the May 1 and its enclosure of the introduction to your company. In view of the high reputation and rich experience of your company in freight forwarding industry, we are willing to appoint your company to be our agent.

Enclosed pleased find:

1. Certificate of Origin No. ZD. 150/03/201

2. Commercial Invoice No. 2589

3. Packing List No. DA650

Your kind cooperation in this respect is greatly appreciated.

Yours faithfully,

Enclosure 1

1. Goods consigned from (export's business name, address, country) NANJING YUNDA IMPORT AND EXPOET CO., LTD. RUIER MANSION RM2103 NO. 75 YUHUA WEST RD, NANJING, CHINA 210005, CHINA	Reference No. ZD. 150/03/201 **GENERALIZED SYSTEM OF PREFERENCE** **CERTIFICATE OF ORIGIN** (Combined declaration and certificate) **FORM A** Issued in <u>THE PEOPLE'S REPUBLIC OF CHINA</u> (country) <div align="right">See Notes Overleaf</div>
2. Goods consigned to (consignee's name, address, country) LOA GENERAL TRADING CO., LTD. P. O. BOX 36654, HAMBURG 22335, GERMANY	
3. Means of Transport and Route (as far as known) From SHANGHAI to HAMBURG by HUITONG 013S on /about JUN 11, 2024	4. For official use **ISSUED RETROSPECTIVELY**

5. Item Number	6. Marks & Numbers of Packages	7. Number and kind of Packages; Description of Goods	8. Origin criterion (see notes overleaf)	9. Gross weight or other quantity	10. Number and date of Invoices
1	LOA GT CK20210026 C/NO. 1-65 HAMBURG	SUCTION FAN IN CARTON TOTAL: SIXTY FIVE (65) CTNS ONLY	P	126KGS	NO. L-2589 MAY 4, 2024

Continued

11. Certification

It is hereby certified, on the basis of control carried out, that the declaration by the exporter is correct.

Shanghai Entry-Exit Inspection and Quarantine Bureau

SHANGHAI, MAY 8, 2024

Place and date, signature and stamp of certifying authority

12. Declaration by the exporter

The undersigned hereby declares that the above details and statements are correct, that all the goods were produced in

CHINA
(country)

and that they comply with the origin requirements specified for those goods in the Generalized System of Preference for goods exported to

GERMANY
(country)

SHANGHAI, MAY 8, 2024

Place and date, signature and stamp of certifying authority

Enclosure 2

NANJING YUNDA IMPORT AND EXPOET CO., LTD.
RUIER MANSION RM2103 NO. 75 YUHUA WEST RD, NANJING, CHINA
TEL: 0086-25-4720998 FAX: 0086-25-4711363

COMMERCIAL INVOICE

No.: L-2589

DATE: MAY 4, 2024

To: M/S LOA GENERAL TRADING CO., LTD.   **Sales Confirmation No.**: CK20240026
　　P. O. BOX 36654, HAMBURG 22335, GERMANY

From: SHANGHAI, CHINA to HAMBURG, GERMANY

Shipped per: HUITONG 013S upon Bill of Lading BL- KLUA0389

Sailing on or about: JUN 11 2024 to HAMBURG, GERMANY

L/C No.: 0011LC243028

Marks & Nos	Description of Goods	Quantities	Unit Price	Amount
LOA GT CK20210026 C/NO. 1-65 HAMBURG,	SUCTION FAN	2000PCS/65CTN	USD 246.00/PCS	USD492,000.00
TOTAL: 65CARTONS/2000PCS CFR DAMMAM PORT, SAUDI ARABIA USD 492,000.00				

NANJING YUNDA IMPORT AND EXPOET CO., LTD.

Signature XXX

Enclosure 3

NANJING YUNDA IMPORT AND EXPOET CO., LTD.

RUILI MANSION RM2103 NO. 75 LUHUQIAO, NANJING, CHINA

PACKING LIST

Sold to: LOA GENERAL TRADING CO., LTD. P. O. BOX 36654, HAMBURG 22335, GERMANY		**No. of Invoice**: L-2589	
^^		**Date**: MAY 4, 2024	
^^		**Reference No.** : CK20240026	
Consignee: AS PER INVOIC		**Country of Origin**: CHINA	
^^		**Country of Destination**: GERMANY	
Shipped per: HUITONG	**Voy. No.** : 013S	**Remarks**:	
SAILING on or about: JUN 11, 2024			
Term of Payment: L/C AT SIGHT			
From: SHANGHAI	**To**: HAMBURG GERMANY		

Marks & No.	Description Goods	Quantity	Packages	Net WGT	Gross WGT	Measurement
LOA GT CK20210026 C/NO. 1-65 HAMBURG	SUCTION FAN	2000PCS	65CTN	90KGs	126KGs	1.544M^3
TOTAL: 2000PCS PACKED IN 65CARTONS 90KGs 126KGs 1.544M^3						

Letter 2　Sending Instruction for Cargo by Sea

May 15, 2024

Dear Sir,

　　We thank you for your letter of May 14 and glad to note that you have accepted the appointment to be our agent to deal with the goods transportation.

　　As you required, we have made out Instruction for Cargo by Sea and checked it carefully to make sure that all the information therein is consistent with L/C. If there is no any problem, please book the shipping space for us.

　　Your prompt reply would be greatly appreciated.

Yours faithfully,

Enclosure:

国际货物海运托运书
INSTRUCTION FOR CARGO BY SEA

合同号 S/C No.	CK20240026	委托编号：Entrustment No.		L-2589
银行编号 Bank No.		信用证号 L/C No.		0011LC243028
开证银行 Opening Bank of L/C	STATE BANK OF GERMANY, HAMBURG, GERMANY	付款方式 Payment Terms		L/C AT SIGHT
托运人 Shipper	\multicolumn{4}{	l	}{NANJING YUNDA IMPORT AND EXPOET CO., LTD. RUIER MANSION RM2103 NO. 75 YUHUA WEST RD, NANJING, CHINA 210005, CHINA TEL：0086-25-4720998 FAX：0086-25-4711363}
收货人 Consignee	\multicolumn{4}{	l	}{TO THE ORDER OF HSH NORDBANK}
通知人 Notify Party	\multicolumn{4}{	l	}{LOA GENERAL TRADING CO., LTD. P. O. BOX 36654, HAMBURG22335, GERMANY TEL：0049-40-3698020 FAX：0049-40-3698021}
贸易性质 Nature of Trading	一般贸易 General Trading	贸易国别 Trading Country	NANJING, CHINA	出口口岸 Export port	SHANGHAI PORT, CHINA
运输方式 Mode of Transport	海运 By sea	消费国别 Consuming Country	GERMANY	目的港 Port of Destination	HAMBURG, GERMANY

Continued

装运期限 Time of Shipment	2024-06-30	可否分批 Partial Shipment	N	运费 Freight	预付 Payable	Y
有效期限 Expiry Date	2024-07-15	可否转运 Transshipment	N		到付 Collect	N

标记及号码 Marks & Nos.	货物名称及描述 Description of Goods	件数 Package No.	毛重 G.W.(kg)	净重 N.W.(kg)	尺码 Meas.(m³)	单价 Unit Price	总价 Amount
LOA GT CK20240026 C/NO. 1-65 HAMBURG	SUCTION FAN	2000PCS/ 65CTN	90kgs	126kgs	1.544m³	USD 246.00 /PCS	USD 492,000.00

Total USD 492,000.00

正本提单 Original B/L	3	副本提单 Copy of B/L	2	价格条件 Payment Terms	CFR HAMBURG, GERMANY	金额币制 Currency	USD

受托人注意事项		指定货代 Freight Forwarder	SHANGHAI YUANTONG INTERNATIONAL TRANSPORTAITON CO.,LTD.
		随附单据 Document Accompanied	发票 Invoice No. L-2589 装箱单 Packing List No. DA650 原产地证书 Certificate of Origin No. ZD.150/03/201

委托人注意事项	保险 Insurance	险别 Risk Insured	ALL RISKS
		保额 Amount Insured	USD 541,200.00
		赔付地点 Claim Payable at	HAMBURG

特殊条款 Special Clauses

备注 Remarks

委托单位盖章 Applicant Stamp & Signature	制单员 Typist	制单日期 Date
NANJING YUNDA IMPORT AND EXPOET CO.,LTD.	LI YONG	2024-05-06

Letter 3 Sending Bill of Lading

May 19, 2024

Dear Sir,

  We are glad to inform you that your consignment of suction fan has now been dispatched as stipulated.

  Enclosed we hand you three Bills of Lading for the goods, per M. S. "HUITONG 013S" to Hamburg. We shall be pleased to hear that the goods will arrive safely and in good order.

  We look forward to the further cooperation between our two companies.

Yours faithfully,

Enclosure:

Shipper NANJING YUNDA IMPORT AND EXPOET CO., LTD. RUIER MANSION RM2103 NO. 75 YUHUA WEST RD, NANJING, CHINA 210005, CHINA	B/L No. SP-01352024 **COSCO** 中国远洋运输公司 CHINA OCEAN SHIPPING COMPANY Combined Transport BILL OF LADING ORIGINAL
Consignee TO THE ORDER OF HSH NORDBANK	SHIPPED on board in apparent good order and condition (unless otherwise indicated) the goods or packages specified herein and to be discharged at the mentioned port of discharge or as near thereto as the vessel may safely get and be always afloat. The weight, measure, marks, numbers, quality, contents and value, being particulars furnished by the Shipper.
Notify Party LOA GENERAL TRADING CO., LTD. P. O. BOX 36654, HAMBURG 22335, GERMANY	The Shipper, Consignee and the Holder of this Bill of loading hereby expressly accept and agree to all printed, written or stamped provisions, exceptions and conditions of this Bill of loading, including those on the back hereof.

Continued

Pre-carriage by	Place of Receipt	Ocean Vessel Voy. No. HUITONG 013S	Port of Loading SHANGHAI	Port of Discharge HAMBURG	Place of Delivery
Container No.	Marks & Nos LOA GT CK20240026 C/NO. 1-65 HAMBURG	Number and Kind of Packages Description of goods SUCTION FAN SIXTY FIVE (65) CTNS TOTAL ONE 20′ CONTAINER CY TO CY FREIGHT PREPAID		Gross Weight 126kgs ON BOARD	Measurement 1.544m³
TOTAL NUMBER OF CONTAINERS (IN WORDS)		SAY SIXTY FIVE CARTONS ONLY			
FREIGHT & CHARGES PREPAID	Revenue Tons	Rate	Per	Prepaid	Collect
	Prepaid at	Payable at		Place and Date of Issue SHANGHAI May. 18, 2024	
Ex. Rate	Total Prepaid	No. of Original B(s)/L THREE(3)		Signed for or on Behalf of the Master XXX	

Practical Usages

1. Enclosing Shipping Documents 寄送运输单据

- Enclosed pleased find: (1)Certificate of Origin No. ZD. 150/03/201; (2)Commercial Invoice No. 2589; (3)Packing List No. DA650.
  随函附寄原产地证书(编号 ZD. 150/03/201)、商业发票(编号 2589),以及装箱单(编号 DA650),请查收。

- As you required, we have made out Instruction for Cargo by Sea and checked it carefully to make sure that all the information therein is consistent with L/C.
  应你方要求,我方已开立货物海运托运书并经仔细核查,以确保每项内容符合信用证规定。

- Enclosed we hand you three Bills of Lading for the goods, per m. s. "HUITONG 013S" to Hamburg.
  现随函附寄由汇通号 013S 发往汉堡的海运提单三份。

2. The Basic Documents in Freight Forwarding Services 货运代理常用单据

- Certificate of Origin 原产地证书
  A certificate of origin (often abbreviated to C/O, COO or CoO) is a document used in international trade. In a printed form or as an electronic document, it is

completed by the exporter and certified by a recognized issuing body, attesting that the goods in a particular export shipment have been produced, manufactured or processed in a particular country.

原产地证书(通常简写为 C/O，COO，或者 CoO)是国际贸易中使用的单据。原产地证书是经出口商填写，由权威机构出具的证明出口货物原产地、制造地或加工地的一种纸质或电子证明文件。

- Commercial Invoice 商业发票

  A commercial invoice is a document required by customs to determine true value of the imported goods for assessment of duties and taxes. A commercial invoice must identify the buyer and seller, and clearly indicate the date and terms of sale, quantity, weight of the shipment, type of packaging, complete description of goods, unit value and total value, and insurance, shipping and other charges.

  商业发票是应海关要求由出口商出具的用以核算进口货物关税的票据。商业发票应载明进出口商名称、销售日期、价格条款、货物数量、重量、包装类型、货物描述、单价与总价、保险、运输以及其他费用。

- Packing List 装箱单

  A packing list is a document prepared by the shipper at the time the goods are shipped, giving the details of invoice, buyer, consignee, country of origin, vessel or flight details, port or airport of loading and discharge, place of delivery, shipping marks, container number, weight and cubic of goods, etc. It is sent to the consignee for accurate tallying of the delivered goods.

  装箱单是托运人在货物装运时出具的单据，通常载明发票信息、购买人、收货人、原产地、船名或航次名、装卸港、交货地、运输标志、装箱数量、货物重量、体积等。装箱单出具后寄送收货人，以便其准确清点到货货物。

- Shipper's Letter of Instruction 货物托运书

  The shipper's letter of instruction is a "letter" from the shipper instructing the freight forwarder how and where to send the export shipment. In preparing this form, the shipper also fills in most of the information required on the Shipper's Export Declaration.

  货物托运书是由托运人向货运代理出具的，指示其如何运输货物且运往哪里的单据。货物托运书的大部分信息是按照出口通关要求填制的。

- Bill of Lading 提单

  A bill of lading is a document issued by a carrier or its agent to the shipper as a contract of carriage of goods. It is also a receipt for cargo accepted for

transportation, and must be presented for taking delivery at the destination.
提单是承运人或其代理人签发给托运人的运输合同,用以表明承运人已接收货物。在目的地提货时必须出示提单。

- Shipping Order 装货单
A shipping order is a document issued to a shipper by the carrier which has accepted the booking note of the shipper for requesting the Captain of the vessel to make the goods on board. A shipping order is one of the most important documents for the exporter or its agent to deal with export customs declaration.
装货单是指接受了托运人提出装运申请的船公司,签发给托运人,凭以命令船长将承运的货物装船的单据。装货单是出口商或其代理人凭以向海关办理出口货物申报手续的重要单据之一。

 Problems Solving

1. Fill in the blanks with the proper words given below.

| packing | transport | transactions | indicate | produced |

Most international trade transactions require some (1) _____ documents, administrative documents, commercial documents and insurance documents. There are a great variety of documents that may need to be (2) _____ to complete export/import transactions; some estimates (3) _____ 200 different documents are used in foreign trade. However, in most export (4) _____, only a few certain documents are used, such as invoice, (5) _____ list and transport document.

2. Work in pairs to discuss what functions the above documents perform in freight services.

Section 4　Skills Training and Case Study Samples

┆ **Skills Training** ┆

A. There are ten incomplete sentences in this part. For each sentence there are three choices marked A, B and C. Choose the one that best completes the sentence.

1. As a receipt, the bill of lading notes that the _____ has received the goods described on the face of document.
　　A. clerk　　　　B. manager　　　　C. carrier
2. Insurance documents refer to some documents related with insurance like

insurance _____.

    A. policy   B. sheet   C. advice

3. Certificate of Origin is certified by a _____ issuing body to attesting that the goods have been produced in a particular country.

    A. recognized   B. mentioned   C. notified

4. The description of the goods in the invoice must _____ with the credit.

    A. comply   B. complete   C. assist

5. We are glad to inform you that the shipment has gone forward and hope that it will arrive at the _____ in perfect condition.

    A. company   B. port   C. destination

6. A commercial invoice is a document required by customs to determine true value of the imported goods for _____ of duties and taxes.

    A. transaction   B. assessment   C. improvement

7. The bill of lading specifies that the carrier is obligated to provide a _____ service in return for a certain charge.

    A. transportation   B. packaging   C. complaining

8. Packing list is sent to the _____ for accurate tallying of the delivered goods.

    A. consignor   B. consignee   C. shipper

9. Straight B/L cannot be _____ to others, while bearer B/L is a kind of negotiable document.

    A. borrowed   B. transferred   C. received

10. The total invoice value should not _____ the total amount of the covering L/C.

    A. exceed   B. except   C. exclude

B. Translate the following terms into English.

原产地证书   装货单

装箱单   货物托运书

提单   商业发票

汇票   支票

航空运单   开票人

C. Translate the following sentences into Chinese.

1. The bill of lading is evidence of the contract of carriage.

2. The main parties on a bill of lading are shipper, consignee, notify party and

carrier.

3. A certificate of origin is a document issued by a certifying authority.
4. The shipping company will tell you when your cargo is loaded on board the ship.
5. Air waybill is not a negotiable document.

Case Study Samples

 Sample 1

"Switch" Bills of Lading

"Switch" bills of lading are a second set of bills of lading issued by the carrier (or by the carrier's agent) in substitution for the set issued at the time of shipment. The agent who is asked to produce the second set is often not at the load port. The holder of the bills may decide, for one reason or another, that the first set of bills is unsuitable, and the carrier is put under commercial pressure to issue switch bills to satisfy his new requirements. Some of these reasons are:

- The original bill names a discharge port which is subsequently changed (perhaps because the goods have been resold);
- A seller of the goods in a chain of contracts does not wish the name of the original shipper to be known;
- The goods were shipped originally in small parcels, and the buyer requires one bill of lading covering all of the parcels to facilitate his on-sale.

The perils of having two sets of bills of lading in circulation for the same cargo are obvious and ship agents must make sure they follow these rules:

- The principal's written authority should be obtained to issue switch bills;
- They should only be issued if the first complete set has been surrendered;
- They should not contain misrepresentations, e.g. as to the true port of loading, or the condition of the cargo. If switch bills contain misrepresentations, the carrier/agent will be at risk of claims from parties who have suffered a loss because of such misrepresentations.

Problems Solving

1. What function does a switch bill of lading perform according to the passage?

2. Are there any risks when ship agents handle a switch B/L? Why?

 Sample 2

Shipper NAN TONG HUAMAO CHEMICAL CORP. YUANDA MANSION RM512 NIHONG WEST RD, TIANJIN, 226200, CHINA	COSCO 中国远洋运输公司 CHINA OCEAN SHIPPING COMPANY	B/L No. COS112024
Consignee TO THE ORDER OF JAPANESE INTERNATIONAL BANK LTD YOKOHAMA BRANCH	ORIGINAL	
Notify Party DCL CHEMICAL CO., LTD. 1306-3 SINCERE BLDG 73-74 NIHON ROAD YOKOHAMA, JAPAN	Combined Transport BILL OF LADING	

Pre-carriage by YANXIN	Place of Receipt NANTONG	Ocean Vessel Voy. No. MCLAY 012D	Port of Loading HONGKONG	Port of Discharge YOKOHAMA	Place of Delivery
Container No.	Marks & Nos T. H. D YOKOHAMA NO. 30000	**Number and Kind of Packages** **Description of goods** TACL IN POWDER 30000 Kraft PAPER BAGs FREIGHT PREPAID		Gross weight 490000KGs	Measurement 390CBM

TOTAL NUMBER OF CONTAINERS (IN WORDS)   SAY THIRTY THOUSAND Kraft PAPER BAGS ONLY

FREIGHT & CHARGES PREPAID Ex. Rate	Revenue Tons	Rate	Per	Prepaid	Collect
	Prepaid at	Payable at		Place and date of Issue NANTONG SEP. 11, 2024 Signed for or on behalf of the Master	
	Total Prepaid	No. of Original B(s)/L THREE (3)			

 Problems Solving

1. What type of the above B/L is?
2. Is the above B/L negotiable? Why?

Section 5 Elevating Vision and Useful Expressions

Elevating Vision

Invoices in Foreign Trade

The types of invoice in foreign trade mainly include proforma invoice, commercial invoice, consular invoice, and customs invoice.

A proforma invoice is a document that states a commitment from the seller to provide specified goods to the buyer at specific prices. It is often used to declare value for customs. It is not a true invoice, because the seller does not record a proforma invoice as an account receivable and the buyer does not record a proforma invoice as an account payable. A proforma invoice is not issued by the seller until the seller and buyer have agreed to the terms of the order. In few cases, proforma invoice is issued for obtaining advance payments from buyer, either for start of production or for security of the goods produced.

A commercial invoice is a document used in foreign trade. It is used as a customs declaration provided by the person or corporation that is exporting an item across international borders. Although there is no standard format, the document must include a few specific pieces of information such as the parties involved in the shipping transaction, the goods being transported, and the country of manufacture. A commercial invoice must also include a statement certifying that the invoice is true, and a signature. A commercial invoice is used to calculate tariffs, international commercial terms (like the Cost in a CIF) and is commonly used for customs purposes.

A consular invoice is a document prepared by a consular official working in the importing country's consulate in the nation of origin. It details the contents of a shipment, and affirms that it does not contain any illegal or questioned items. The document is written in the language used by the importing country to ensure that customs officials can read and understand it, and includes a seal confirming that it is official. Such documents may be required for some imports, and can be recommended in other cases. Customs officials use this document to determine appropriate tariffs, duties, and other fees in association with a shipment.

A customs invoice is a document required by the customs in some import countries.

It is mainly used as a foundation for customs statistics, taxation and certifying the origin of the goods, making sure whether there is dumping tendency.

 Useful Expression

货运单据术语	
airway bill 航空运单	mate's receipt 收货单/大副收据
booking note 托运单	multimodal transport document (MTD) 多式运输单据
certificate of origin (C/O) 原产地证书	negotiable instrument 可转让票据
certificate of quality 品质证明书	on board B/L 已装船提单
charter party B/L 租船提单	on deck B/L 舱面提单
combined transport B/L 联合运输提单	packing list 装箱单
destination 目的地	proforma invoice (P/L) 形式发票
direct B/L 直达提单	railway bill 铁路运单
drawee 受票人	seaway bill 海运运单
drawer 出票人	shipping advice 装船通知
duplicate 副本	shipping documents 货运单证
endorsor 背书人	shipping order (S/O) 装货单/关单/下货纸
freight collect B/L 运费到付提单	stale B/L 过期提单
freight prepaid B/L 运费预付提单	through B/L 联运提单
import license 进口许可证	transshipment B/L 转船提单
insurance certificate 保险凭证	triplicate 一式三份
insurance policy 保险单	
liner B/L 班轮提单	

Unit 9

Commodity Inspection

Learning Objectives

- To know the procedure of commodity inspection
- To know the main laws and regulations in commodity inspection
- To learn the key words and expressions of commodity inspection

Skill Developing Objectives

- To develop communication skills in commodity inspection
- To develop writing skills in commodity inspection

Section 1 Theme Lead-in

Read the following passage to get a better understanding of this unit.

The Measures of the People's Republic of China for the Administration of Import and Export Food Safety

Article 57 The General Administration of Customs, based on Article 100 of the Food Safety Law, collects and summarizes the safety information about import and export food, and sets up a safety information management system for import and export food. The Customs Administrations at all levels take charge of collecting and sorting out the safety information about import and export food within their jurisdictions and designated by the Customs Administration at the superior level, and, based on relevant provisions, notify the local governments, relevant authorities, institutions and enterprises in their jurisdictions. In case that the information notified involves other regions, a notice should be given also to the Customs Administration in relevant regions. In addition to the contents required by Article 100 of the Food Safety Law, the safety information about import and export food collected and summarized by the Customs Administration should also include the information about technical measures to trade food in foreign countries.

Article 58 The Customs Administration should conduct risk research and judgment on the collected safety information about the import and export food, and, based on the relevant results, determine the corresponding control measures.

Article 59 In case of an outbreak of food safety incidents or epidemics at home and abroad that may affect import and export food safety, or any serious food safety issues discovered in the import and export food, the Customs Administration directly under the General Administration should immediately file a report to the General Administration of Customs. The General Administration of Customs shall, depending on the developments, release a risk alert, render a risk warning notice within the system of the Customs Administration, notify the department of the State Council responsible for food safety supervision and management, health administrative and agricultural administrative departments, and, if necessary, give a risk warning notice to consumers. For the import and export food with a risk warning notice given by the General Administration of Customs, the control measures stipulated in Article 34, Article 35, Article 36 and Article 54 of these Measures shall be taken according to the requirements specified in the risk warning notice.

Article 60 The Customs Administration formulates an annual national schedule to monitor safety risks in import and export food, and collect monitoring data and relevant information related to food-borne diseases, food contamination and harmful factors in the import and export food in a systematic and consistent manner.

Notes

1. The General Administration of Customs, based on Article 100 of the Food Safety Law, collects and summarizes the safety information about import and export food, and sets up a safety information management system for import and export food.
海关总署依据《食品安全法》第一百条,收集汇总进出口食品安全信息,并建立进出口食品安全信息管理系统。

2. The Customs Administrations at all levels take charge of collecting and sorting out the safety information about import and export food within their jurisdictions and designated by the Customs Administration at the superior level, and, based on relevant provisions, notify the local governments, relevant authorities, institutions and enterprises in their jurisdictions.
各级海关负责收集整理本辖区以及上级海关指定的进出口食品安全信息,并依据相关规定,向本辖区的地方政府、有关部门、机构和企业通报。

3. In addition to the contents required by Article 100 of the Food Safety Law, the safety information about import and export food collected and summarized by the Customs Administration should also include the information about technical measures to trade food in foreign countries.
除《食品安全法》第一百条要求的内容外,海关收集汇总的进出口食品安全信息还应包括国外对食品贸易采取的技术措施信息。

4. The Customs Administration should conduct risk research and judgment on the collected safety information about the import and export food, and, based on the relevant results, determine the corresponding control measures.
海关应对收集的进出口食品安全信息进行风险研究和判断,并根据相关结果确定相应的控制措施。

5. In case of an outbreak of food safety incidents or epidemics at home and abroad that may affect import and export food safety, or any serious food safety issues

discovered in the import and export food, the Customs Administration directly under the General Administration should immediately file a report to the General Administration of Customs.

国内外发生食品安全事故或者流行病学情况可能影响进出口食品安全，或者发现严重进出口食品安全问题的，直属海关应当立即向海关总署报告。

6. The General Administration of Customs shall, depending on the developments, release a risk alert, render a risk warning notice within the system of the Customs Administration, notify the department of the State Council responsible for food safety supervision and management, health administrative and agricultural administrative departments, and, if necessary, give a risk warning notice to consumers.

海关总署根据情况，发布风险预警通告，向国务院食品安全监督管理、卫生行政、农业行政部门通报，并视情况向消费者发布风险警示通告。

7. For the import and export food with a risk warning notice given by the General Administration of Customs, the control measures stipulated in Article 34, Article 35, Article 36 and Article 54 of these Measures shall be taken according to the requirements specified in the risk warning notice.

海关总署发布风险预警通告的进出口食品，按照风险预警通告的要求，依照本办法第三十四条、第三十五条、第三十六条、第五十四条的规定采取控制措施。

8. The Customs Administration formulates an annual national schedule to monitor safety risks in import and export food, and collect monitoring data and relevant information related to food-borne diseases, food contamination and harmful factors in the import and export food in a systematic and consistent manner.

海关制定年度进出口食品安全风险监测计划，系统和持续地收集进出口食品中食源性疾病、食品污染和有害因素的监测数据及相关信息。

 Problems Solving

1. Work in pairs to discuss the comprehensive approach taken by the General Administration of Customs to ensure the safety of import and export food as outlined in Articles 57-60.

2. Decide whether the following statement is true or false according to the passage.

(1) The General Administration of Customs is responsible for collecting and summarizing safety information about import and export food according to Article 100 of the Food Safety Law.　　　　　　　　　　　　　　　　　　　　　( )

(2) If the notified safety information involves other regions, there is no need to inform the Customs Administration in those relevant regions.　　　　　　　(　　)

(3) The safety information collected by the Customs Administration does not need to include information about technical measures to trade food in foreign countries.

(　　)

(4) The Customs Administration should determine control measures based on the results of risk research and judgment on the collected safety information about import and export food.　　　　　　　　　　　　　　　　　　　　　　　　(　　)

(5) When serious food safety issues are discovered in import and export food, the General Administration of Customs must immediately issue a risk warning notice to consumers.　　　　　　　　　　　　　　　　　　　　　　　　　　　　(　　)

Section 2　Conversations and Warm-up

+-+-+-+-+-+-+
Conversations
+-+-+-+-+-+-+

 Conversation 1　Commodity Inspection

(*A is Wang Jing, a freight forwarder and B is John Smith, an exporter. They are talking about the commodity inspection.*)

A: Good morning, Mr. Smith.

B: Good morning, Mr. Wang. We have settled the transportation issue in the previous talk. Today, let's take up the question of inspection.

A: Okay. As an integral part of the contract, the inspection of goods has its special importance.

B: Yes. Our goods will be inspected by Tianjin Entry-Exit Inspection and Quarantine Bureau.

A: We agreed on that. But remember that you should provide with other documents, a certificate of quantity and fumigation.

B: Of course. The Inspection Certificate will be signed by the commissioner of the Bureau.

A: You know, if the quantity of the goods does not conform to that stipulated in the contract, we will refuse to accept the goods.

B: All right. If there should be any disputes, we wish to have them settled through friendly discussions.

Conversation 2   Commodity Inspection's Importance

(*A and B, who are the staff in different companies, are communicating with the commodity inspection.*)

A: In the previous talk we have settled transportation issue, and today let's take up the question of inspection.

B: We appreciate your work efficiency. As an integral part of the contract, the inspection of goods has its special importance.

A: Yes. Inspection is of vital importance in international trade. Our goods will be inspected by China Import and Export Commodity Inspection Bureau or by any of its branches.

B: We agreed on that. But remember that you should provide with other documents such as a certificate of quantity and fumigation.

A: Of course. The Inspection Certificate will be signed by the commissioner of the bureau.

B: If the quantity of the goods does not conform to that stipulated in the contract, we will refuse to accept the goods.

A: All right, if there should be any disputes, we wish to have them settled through friendly discussions.

B: I share the same idea.

A. Well, it seems that we have covered everything.

A: Good.

 Conversation 3   Declaring Hair Dryer

(*A is a Inspection affairs officer and B is a consignor.*)

A: Good morning. What goods will you export to Germany?

B: Hair dryer.

A: Have you obtained the Certificate of Approval?

B: Yes, here you are.

A: Sorry. The Certificate of Approval is made by the factory. You have to get the Certificate of Approval signed by the technique Center of Entry-Exit Inspection and Quarantine Bureau.

B: How could I get it?

A: First, you should go to the Inspection Affairs Office to apply for declaration; then you should send a sample of hair dryer to the Technique Center of Entry-

Exit Inspection and Quarantine Bureau. If the quality of your goods were eligible, you would get the Certificate of Approval.

B: What should I do next?

A: We will inspect your hair dryers and if the number and quality of the hair dryers were the same as the terms stipulated in the contract, then you could export them.

B: I see. Thank you for your explanation.

 Warm-up

A. Match the definitions in Column B with the terms in Column A.

A	B
1. inspection	A. be in line with
2. quarantine	B. a formal or official examination
3. conform	C. required by rule
4. sterilize	D. isolation to prevent the spread of infectious disease
5. compulsory	E. make free from bacteria

B. The following is a passage about commodity inspection. Fill in the blanks with the words given in the box and discuss with your partners about the importance of commodity inspection in foreign trade.

manner   authorized   transaction   transfer   delivered

Commodity inspection is an indispensable link in the chain of smooth handling of foreign trade (1) _____. The commodity inspection is the inspection conducted by a third (2) _____ party with the purpose of testifying whether a commodity's quality, quantity package, etc., would be as same as the terms stipulated in the contract. In international trade, the quality and quantity of the goods (3) _____ by the seller should be in conformity with the terms of the contract and should be packed in the (4) _____ required by the contract. In this case, inspection of commodity and the insurance of certificate of inspection are necessary steps in the (5) _____ of the goods.

C. Make up a dialogue according to the following situation.

Student A works as an inspection affairs officer, and Student B is an Entry-Exit Inspection and Quarantine Declarer. Student A and Student B will act out the dialogue of commodity inspection.

The dialogue should cover the following information: the goods being declared, the certificate of approval, and the customs clearance form of goods.

Section 3 Format Writings and Practical Usages

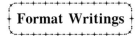

After reading the following passage, you are required to discuss with your partners and to complete the statements that follow the questions.

Plant Protection and Quarantine Permits

Plant Protection and Quarantine (PPQ) is a program within the Animal and Plant Health Inspection Service (APHIS), an agency of the United States Department of Agriculture (USDA). The PPQ program attempts to safeguard agriculture and natural resources in the United States of America against the entry, establishment, and spread of animal and plant pests and noxious weeds. PPQ also supports trade and exports of U.S. agricultural products.

Any person interested in moving a regulated article needs to obtain a PPQ permit. A permit is a written or electronic authorization that allows, under prescribed conditions, the movement of regulated articles, including: plants, plant products, biological control organisms, plant pests, noxious weeds, items that may harbor these organisms, or means of conveyance.

APHIS requires permits under the authority of the Plant Protection Act of 2000, in order to help safeguard the health of U.S. agricultural and natural resources. For example, import permits are required for the entry and transit through the United States of agricultural products that pose a risk of introducing exotic plant pests and diseases. Additionally, import permits are necessary for the movement of plants whose populations are threatened in the wild and are protected by the Convention on International Trade in Endangered Species of Wild Fauna and Flora (CITES).

When making decisions concerning permit requests, PPQ carefully weighs the potential risks and benefits of the request and reviews the related scientific information.

 Problems Solving

1. What is a PPQ permit?
2. According to the passage, what articles are required to obtain a PPQ permit?
3. What are the functions of a PPQ permit?

4. Are plant protection and quarantine permits important in foreign trade? Why?

 Writing Samples

Letter 1 Inspection Clauses

May 15, 2024

Dear Sir,

In the previous letter, we have mutually agreed that the goods are subject to the Inspection Certificate of Quality and Inspection Certificate of Quantity issued by Shanghai Entry-Exit Inspection and Quarantine Bureau at the port of shipment.

We would like to mention that any discrepancy on the shipped goods should be put forward within 30 days after the arrival of the vessel carrying the goods at the port of destination and the Survey Report issued by the Surveyor we agreed should be presented.

Yours faithfully,

Letter 2 Inspection Certificate

May 25, 2024

Dear Sir,

We are very glad to have received your letter of May 24, in which you would like to know the details of inspection.

As we have agreed, inspection will be carried out by Shanghai Entry-Exit Inspection and Quarantine Bureau before shipment. The Survey Report issued by Shanghai Entry-Exit Inspection and Quarantine Bureau may be taken as the basis for negotiating documents. After the goods arrive at the destination, the consignee has the right of re-inspection. The inspection certificate of his surveyor will serve as the basis for lodging a claim.

The Certificate of Inspection will be made out in Chinese and English.

If there is any discrepancy on inspection, please don't hesitate to contact us.

Yours faithfully,

Practical Usages

1. Inspection Clauses 检验条款

- We have mutually agreed that the goods are subject to the Inspection Certificate of Quality and Inspection Certificate of Quantity issued by Shanghai Entry-Exit Inspection and Quarantine Bureau at the port of shipment.
  双方同意以装运港上海出入境检验检疫局签发的品质及数量检验证书为最后依据。

- We would like to mention that any discrepancy on the shipped goods should be put forward within 30 days after the arrival of the vessel carrying the goods at the port of destination and the Survey Report issued by the Surveyor we agreed should be presented.
  我们想提醒贵公司，对于装运货物的任何异议必须与装运货物的船只到达目的港后30日内提出，并须提供经双方同意的公证机关出具的检验报告。

- After the goods arrive at the destination, the consignee has the right of re-inspection.
  货物到达目的港后，收货人有权复验。

- Inspection will be carried out by Shanghai Entry-Exit Inspection and Quarantine Bureau before shipment.
  由上海出入境检验检疫局进行装船前检验。

2. Inspection Certificate 检验证书

- The Survey Report issued by Shanghai Entry-Exit Inspection and Quarantine Bureau may be taken as the basis for negotiating documents.
  上海出入境检验检疫局的检验报告可以作为议付的依据。

- The inspection certificate of his surveyor will serve as the basis for lodging a claim.
  其检验机构出具的检验证书可作为索赔的依据。

- The Certificate of Inspection will be made out in Chinese and English.
  检验证书用中文与英文开具。

- Before delivery the manufacturer should make a precise and overall inspection of the goods regarding quality, quantity, specification and performance and issue the certificate indicating the goods in conformity with the stipulation of the contract.
  在交货前制造商应就订货的质量、规格、数量、性能做出准确全面的检验，并出具货物与本合同相符的检验证书。
- The products applying for the quality license should meet the compulsory requirements of the national technical specifications.
申请质量许可证的产品必须符合国家技术规范的强制性要求。

 Problems Solving

1. Suppose you have received the above Letter 1 and have some discrepancy on inspection clauses. Write a letter to express your suggestions.
2. The following is a passage about inspection. Fill in the blanks with the words given below.

| written | conformity | specification | negotiation | inspection |

Before delivery the manufacturer should make a precise and overall (1)_____ of the goods regarding quality, quantity, (2)_____ and performance and issue the certificate indicating the goods in (3)_____ with the stipulation of the contract. The certificates are one part of the documents presented to the bank for (4)_____ of the payment and should not be considered as final regarding quality, quantity, specification and performance. The manufacturer should include the inspection (5)_____ report in the Inspection Certificate of Quality, stating the inspection particulars.

Section 4　Skills Training and Case Study Samples

Skills Training

A. There are ten incomplete sentences in this part. For each sentence there are three choices marked A, B and C. Choose the one that best completes the sentence.

1. Commodity inspection is a/an _____ link in the chain of smooth handling of foreign trade transaction.

　　A. indispensable　　B. credible　　C. releasable

2. The quality and quantity of the goods delivered by the seller should be in _____ with the terms of the contract.

　　A. correct　　B. conformity　　C. conduct

3. If the quality of your goods were _____, you would get the Certificate of Approval.

　　A. specific　　B. suitable　　C. eligible

4. Any person interested in moving a regulated article needs to _____ a permit.

   A. obtain   B. inspect   C. effect

5. Inspection will be carried _____ by Shanghai Entry-Exit Inspection and Quarantine Bureau before shipment.

   A. up   B. in   C. out

6. The Survey Report issued by Shanghai Entry-Exit Inspection and Quarantine Bureau may be taken as the basis for documents _____.

   A. discussing   B. negotiating   C. issuing

7. The Certificate of Inspection will be made out _____ English.

   A. at   B. in   C. on

8. The inspection certificates are one part of the documents _____ to the bank.

   A. accepted   B. endorsed   C. presented

9. The Customs shall check and _____ the commodities on the strength of the customs clearance form of goods.

   A. release   B. reject   C. object

10. The consignee can apply to the authorities for inspection within the time limit as _____ uniformly by the GAQSIQ

    A. deducted   B. prescribed   C. expected

B. Translate the following terms into English.

法定检验   批准文件
出入境检验检疫机构   复验
验证管理   检验证书
货物通关单   异议
换证凭单   公证机关

C. Translate the following sentences into Chinese.

1. The inspection of the import and export commodities which are listed in the Catalogue shall be conducted by the commodity inspection authorities.

2. The consignee or his agent shall apply for inspection to the commodity inspection authorities located at the place he makes Customs declarations.

3. The Customs shall check and release the commodities on the strength of the Documents for Customs Clearance issued by the commodity inspection authorities.

4. No permission shall be granted for loading and shipment until the vessel holds or containers have passed the inspection.

5. When going through the formalities of applying for inspection, the agent shall submit his letter of authorization to the commodity inspection authorities.

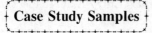

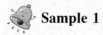 **Sample 1**

Import Permits of Quarantine

(Excerpt from Implementing Regulations for the Law of the People's Republic of China on Import and Export Commodity Inspection)

The following objects must be submitted for import permits of quarantine:

(1) List of animals required for import permits of quarantine:
- Live animals: animals (whether domesticated or wild, such as livestock, poultry, beasts, snakes, tortoises, fishes, shrimps and prawns, crabs, shellfishes, silkworms and bees), embryos, semen, oosperm, propagating eggs, and other animal hereditary materials;
- Animal products used for food: meat and meat products (including the viscera), fresh eggs, fresh milk;
- Animal products not used for food: bones, hoofs, horns and their products, glutin, cocoons, feedstuff from animals and foodstuff additive, fishmeal, meat meal, bone meal, meat and bone meal, grease, blood meal, blood, etc., organic fertilizers containing elements from animals.

(2) List of plants required for import permits of quarantine:
- Plant propagating materials: seeds, seedlings and other live plants;
- Fruits and vegetables: fresh fruits, tomatoes, eggplants, fruit of capsicum;
- Tobaccos: tobacco leaves and tobacco flakes;
- Grains and cereals: wheat, corns, paddies, barleys, ryes, oats, broom corns, etc. ;
- Tuber crops: potatoes, cassavas, sweet potatoes;
- Feedstuff: mill feed, bean cakes, bean hull, peanut hull, vegetable seed hull, etc. ;
- Others: plant culture materials.

(3) Carriers of the above-mentioned animal and plant products shall apply to

GDCIQ for import permits of quarantine. Lists of exhibitions and relevant exhibition documents shall be submitted. GDCIQ shall be in charge of verification, and AQSIQ shall be in charge of approval.

 Problems Solving

1. What articles are required for import permits of quarantine? Make a three-minute presentation to make an introduction. You can use some visual aid to help you to express yourself, such as a flowchart, a diagram or a PPT.
2. Suppose you work as a freight forwarder. Write a letter to your client who is willing to export some grains to Germany. Tell him the procedures and tips for entry-exit inspection and quarantine.

 Sample 2

Quality License for Export Commodities

1. Licensing Conditions

(1) The applicant should enjoy the independent legal entity qualification.

(2) The applicant should have effective quality assurance system in place.

(3) The products applying for the quality license should meet the compulsory requirements of the national technical specifications. If such requirements are not established yet, you may refer to the related standards as designated by the administrative department for the quality license system of export commodities.

2. Procedures

(1) The applicant should apply to the local acceptance body and submit the relevant materials.

(2) The acceptance body shall, based on the completeness and compliance with legal form of the submitted materials, decide whether to accept the application or not, and issue a written document as prescribed.

(3) After accepting the application, the acceptance body shall take and seal the samples from the applied products, which will be sent by the applicant to the designated testing body for type testing. After receiving the qualified product type-testing report, the acceptance body will organize the audit team to carry out on-site audit on the plant quality assurance system.

(4) Shanghai Entry-Exit Inspection and Quarantine Bureau will decide whether to approve licensing or not on the basis of the application materials, type testing report and the results of on-site audit. If the licensing is approved, SHCIQ will issue the Quality License for Export Commodities within 10 workdays. If not, the Decision of No Administrative Licensing will be issued.

 Problems Solving

1. What licensing conditions are required for the application for Quality License for Export Commodities?
2. Make a three-minute presentation to introduce the licensing procedures of Quality License for Export Commodities. You can use some visual aid to help you to express yourself, such as a flowchart, a diagram or a PPT.

 ## Section 5 Elevating Vision and Useful Expressions

Elevating Vision

Inspection of Import Commodities
(Excerpt from the Law of the People's Republic of China on Import and Export Commodity Inspection)

Article 11 For import commodities which are subject to inspection by the commodity inspection authorities, as provided for by this Law, the consignee or his agent shall apply for inspection to the commodity inspection authorities located at the place he makes Customs declarations. The Customs shall check and release the commodities on the strength of the Documents for Customs Clearance issued by the commodity inspection authorities.

Article 12 For import commodities which are subject to inspection by the commodity inspection authorities, as provided for by this Law, the consignee or his agent shall, in the places and within the time limit specified by the commodity inspection authorities, accept inspection of the import commodities conducted by the commodity inspection authorities. The commodity inspection authorities shall complete the inspection and issue an inspection certificate within the time limit specified uniformly by the State administration for commodity inspection.

Article 13 Where the consignee of the import commodities other than those that are subject to inspection by the commodity inspection authorities, as provided for by this Law, finds that the import commodities do not meet the relevant quality requirements, are damaged or are short on weight or quantity, he shall apply to the commodity inspection authorities for inspection and the issuance of an inspection certificate if such a certificate is necessary for claiming compensation.

Article 14 For important import commodities and complete sets of equipment in large size, the consignee shall, in accordance with the terms agreed upon in foreign trade contracts, conduct initial inspection or initial supervision over manufacturing or loading in the exporting country before shipment, over which the relevant competent departments shall tighten their supervision. The commodity inspection authorities may, when necessary, dispatch inspection officials to take part in such inspection and supervision.

 Useful Expression

商 检 用 语	
Animal Health Certificate 动物卫生证书	IEC 国际电工委员会
ANSI 美国国家标准协会	IPPC 国际植物保护公约
CCC 中国强制认证	ISO 国际标准化组织
Certificate of Fumigation 熏蒸证书	ITU 国际电信联盟
Certificate of Health 健康证书	IWTO 国际毛纺组织
Certificate of Origin 产地证书	OIE 世界动物卫生组织
Certificate of Packing 包装证书	Phytosanitary Certificate 植物检疫证书
Certificate of Quality 品质证书	Quarantine Certificate for Conveyance 运输工具检疫证书
Certificate of Quantity 数量证书	
Certificate of Quarantine 检疫证书	Sanitary Certificate 卫生证书
Certificate of Weight 重量证书	SPS 实施动植物卫生检疫措施协议
CIQ 中国检验检疫	TBT 技术性贸易壁垒协议
CQC 中国进出口质量认证中心	Veterinary Certificate 兽医证书
FAO 联合国粮农组织	Veterinary Health Certificate 兽医卫生证书
FEIS 美国食品安全检验局	WHO 国际卫生组织
Fumigation/Disinfection Certificate 熏蒸/消毒证书	WTO 世界贸易组织
ICAO 国际民航组织	

Unit 10

Customs Clearance

Learning Objectives

- To know the procedure of customs clearance
- To understand the basic documents for customs clearance
- To learn the key words and expression in customs clearance

Skill Developing Objectives

- To develop communication skills in customs clearance
- To develop writing skills in customs clearance

Section 1　Theme Lead-in

Read the following passage to get a better understanding of this unit.

Facilitative Customs Clearance Measures

Facilitative customs clearance measures mainly include customs declarations in advance, networking declaration, rapid transit, door to door inspection and release, urgent customs clearance and release with customs security.

Customs declarations in advance

To shorten the operating hours of customs clearance, these enterprises can, in the case that the description, the specifications and the quantity of the import and export goods are determinate, declare to the customs in advance and submit related documents after import goods shipped and before arriving or within three days before export goods carried to the customs surveillance zone. Customs shall directly examine and release the goods after arrival of the goods.

Networking declaration

In their offices, the enterprises shall apply China E-Port platform and directly declare to the customs at the place where the goods enter the territory or the competent customs. The enterprises shall input all customs data once only. Therefore, the data shall transmit through network among import and export management departments. Customs examines the declaration electronic data and send electronic return receipt by which document audit and cargo clearance procedures may be made by the enterprises themselves or their entrusted agents in the customs clearance spot. Some customs in good condition shall collect duties by nominated bank online. Customs issues electronic payment notice to the enterprise, and release the goods based on the electronic return receipt of bank transfers.

Rapid transit

According to the requirements of above-mentioned enterprises, customs shall give priority to their goods imported and exported in the different domestic ports (not including the goods that the state designate the ports to import/export), to go through customs formalities of rapid transit transportation.

Door-to-door inspection and release

To the import/export goods that shall be examined but are not convenient to be examined in customs clearance spot, customs shall, basing on the requirements of the enterprises, give priority to dispatching members to examine the goods in the link of combined production or loading/unloading.

Urgent customs clearance

Customs gives priority to auditing to the import/export goods of above-mentioned enterprises. In the customs clearance spot with excessive import/export goods, customs shall establish "to facilitate customs clearance" window to go through customs formalities in advance. These enterprises can contact with the competent customs through an appointment for customs clearance procedures during working hours and holidays.

Release with customs securities

Because of a temporary inability to provide certain documents (not including import and export license documents) or other information, customs are unable to identify the goods classification, assessment of value and other customs clearance conditions resulting in unpunctual examination and release of the goods. To solve such problems, customs shall allow above-mentioned enterprises to go through customs formalities in advance, in the form of securities recognized by the customs, and to add on the document or information and pay duties or go through other procedures after a specified period of time.

 Notes

1. Facilitative customs clearance measures mainly include customs declarations in advance, networking declaration, rapid transit, door to door inspection and release, urgent customs clearance and release with customs security.
便利通关措施主要包括提前报关、联网报关、快速转关、上门验放、加急通关、担保验放等。

2. To shorten the operating hours of customs clearance, these enterprises can, in the case that the description, the specifications and the quantity of the import and export goods are determinate, declare to the customs in advance and submit related documents after import goods shipped and before arriving or within three days before export goods carried to the customs surveillance zone.
为缩短进出口货物通关时间,上述企业可在进口货物起运后抵港前、出口货物运入海关监管场所前三日内,在能够确定其进出口货物的品名、规格、数量的情况下,提前向海关办理报关手续并递交有关单证。

3. In their offices, the enterprises shall apply China E-Port platform and directly

declare to the customs at the place where the goods enter the territory or the competent customs.

企业应用中国电子口岸平台，在企业办公地点直接向进出口地或主管地海关自行办理正式报关手续。

4. Customs examines the declaration electronic data and send electronic return receipt by which document audit and cargo clearance procedures may be made by the enterprises themselves or their entrusted agents in the customs clearance spot.

海关审核报关单电子数据后发送电子回执，由企业自行派人或委托代理人在货物通关现场向海关办理交单审核及货物验放手续。

5. To the import/export goods that shall be examined but are not convenient to be examined in customs clearance spot, customs shall, basing on the requirements of the enterprises, give priority to dispatching members to examine the goods in the link of combined production or loading/unloading.

对应当查验又不便在通关现场查验的进出口货物，海关应根据上述企业要求，优先派员到企业结合生产或装卸环节实施查验。

6. In the customs clearance spot with excessive import/export goods, customs shall establish "to facilitate customs clearance" window to go through customs formalities in advance.

上述企业进出口货物较多的通关现场，海关应设立便捷通关窗口优先办理货物验放手续。

7. Because of a temporary inability to provide certain documents (not including import and export license documents) or other information, customs are unable to identify the goods classification, assessment of value and other customs clearance conditions resulting in unpunctual examination and release of the goods.

在办理通关手续时，因企业暂时无法提供某些单证（不包括进出口许可证件）或其他信息，海关无法确定货物的商品归类、估价等结关条件从而导致不能及时验放货物。

 Problems Solving

1. Work in pairs to discuss the procedure of customs clearance.
2. Decide whether the following statement is true or false according to the passage.
(1) The enterprises can declare to the customs within five days before export goods

carried to the customs surveillance zone. (   )

(2) The enterprises cannot directly declare to the customs at their offices. (   )

(3) Customs shall establish "to facilitate customs clearance" window in the customs clearance spot with excessive import/export goods. (   )

(4) Customs examines the declaration electronic data and send paper return receipt to the enterprises. (   )

(5) To the goods that are not convenient to be examined in customs clearance spot, customs shall give priority to dispatching members to examine the goods, basing on the requirements of the enterprises. (   )

Section 2　Conversations and Warm-up

Conversations

 Conversation 1　Introduction to Customs

(A is a freight forwarder, who is talking with B, a business man who wants to know something about customs.)

A: Could you tell me the functions of customs?

B: The customs of a country shall be a state organ responsible for supervision and control over everything entering and leaving the customs territory.

A: Everything? Including personal belongings?

B: Right. The customs establishments shall exercise supervision and control over goods, means of transport, passenger's luggage and personal articles.

A: I know the customs also collect customs duties and other taxes and fees.

B: Yes. Besides these, the tasks of the customs also include preventing smuggling activities, compiling customs statistics and dealing with other customs matters.

A: I see. How many customs establishments are there in China?

B: I am not sure. You know with the development of China's external economy and trade, more and more customs establishments are set up. Maybe today, there is a new one established.

 Conversation 2　Applying for Customs Declaration

(A, Li Jing, is a consigner, who is applying for customs declaration. Now she is communicating with B, who is a customs officer.)

B: Hello, the Customs. How can I help you?

A: Good morning! This is Li Jing, a consigner applying for declaration. I have some troubles in the declaration procedure.

B: Okay, what's the matter?

A: Well, I'm afraid there's a mistake that the unit price and total price of my goods in the export declaration are changed. They're different from what I filled in the declaration.

B: Oh. There is a problem. Let me check it for you. What is the number of your declaration?

A: 678932. Thank you!

B: The unit price and total price have been changed, but...

A: But why?

B: The price you filled was too low, so we have it reassessed. That is the reason you find it distinct.

A: Well, how could it be that low?

B: There is a regulation that the unit price of this sort of goods can't be lower than $30 and higher than $100, and the price you filled in was $25.

A: I see. But it needn't be that much as $95. It is much too high. Can I just raise the price to $30? So that it could meet the regulation.

B: Okay. But it takes about two days to change it and documents attached.

A: All right. Should I do anything else?

B: Let me see. The taxes would also change, and you have to pay taxes due to the new price.

A: Fine. Thank you for your help!

B: Never mind.

 Conversation 3 Tips for Customs Clearance

(*A and B are continuing their conversation.*)

A: What preparations should be made before the customs clearance?

B: Prior to the landing of the goods, all the documents and invoices required for customs declaration should be prepared and checked before submission to the customs officer or agent for declaration purposes.

A: Anything else?

B: And a sum equivalent to the amount of customs duty chargeable on the import goods should also be made available.

A: I see. What should I pay attention to during the process of customs clearance?

B: Throughout the process of customs clearance, you need to keep in close contact with the customs officer or agent and promptly provide any documents required, such as product manual, copy of letter of credit and quarantine certificate, trade agreement, etc.

A: That's really important.

B: One more thing. Upon inspection and release by the customs, the import goods should be promptly delivered or transferred in order to minimize warehousing or transfer charges.

A: I've got it. Thank you very much.

 Warm-up

A. Match the definitions in Column B with the terms in Column A.

A	B
1. customs	A. the product specific number used to classify the goods
2. commodity code	B. a document certified by an recognized issuing body attesting that the goods have been manufactured in a particular country
3. certificate of origin	C. the place where people have to declare goods that they bring with them
4. tariff	D. management by overseeing the performance or operation of a person or group
5. supervision	E. a tax that a government collects on goods coming into a country

B. The following is a passage about customs. Fill in the blanks with the words given in the box and then discuss with your partners about the functions of customs.

| illegal   agency   bonded   cleared   quotas |

Customs is a general term for an (1) _____ in a country responsible for controlling the flow of goods into the country. Customs agencies attempt to prevent dangerous, hazardous or (2) _____ materials from entering the country, and also collect tariff and other taxes. They may also enforce import (3) _____. In most countries, customs are attained through government agreements and international laws. A customs duty is a tariff or tax on the importation or exportation of goods. Commercial goods not yet (4) _____ through customs are held in a customs area, often called a (5) _____ store, until processed.

C. Make up a dialogue according to the following situation.

Student A works as a clerk in a customs agency, and Student B is a freight forwarder. Student A and Student B will act out the dialogue about customs clearance.

The dialogue should cover the following information: the functions of customs, the documents required in the progress of customs clearance and the time limit to the payment for customs duties.

Section 3 Format Writings and Practical Usages

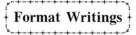

After reading the following passage, you are required to discuss with your partners and to complete the statements that follow the questions.

Import and Export Declaration

In the mainland of China, import and export declarations should be lodged before cargoes are released. In other countries or regions, they may be submitted within a prescribed period after shipment.

The typical types of information required in import and export declarations include identifying of the exporter/importer, description of the goods, mode of transport, CIF or FOB value, etc.

In China, import declaration consists of three basic steps: (1) Filling out the declaration form; (2) Inspection of the goods and the accompanying documents by customs officials; (3) Release/clearance from customs after payment of the customs duties or taxes.

The usual types of the documents required for import clearance are import cargo declaration form, import license, export cargo inspection form, packing list, bill of lading or air waybill, commercial invoice, declaration of non-wood packaging, and the document on the basis of which tax reduction or waiver of inspection is claimed.

The usual types of accompanying documents required for export clearance include export cargo declaration form, export cargo inspection form, shipping order, bill of lading or air waybill, commercial invoice, packing list, certificate of origin and foreign exchange settlement certificate.

Problems Solving

1. When should import and export declaration be lodged in the Chinese mainland?

2. What types of information are required in import and export declarations?
3. How many steps does import declaration consist of?
4. What documents are required for import clearance?
5. What documents are required for export clearance?

Writing Samples

Letter 1 Export Customs Declaration Form

中华人民共和国海关出口货物报关单
EXPORT CUSTOMS DECLARATION FORM OF THE
PEOPLE'S REPUBLIC OF CHINA

预录入编号: 海关编号:
No. of pre-record: No. of customs:

出口口岸 Port of export:	备案号 Record filing No.:	出口日期 Date of export:	申报日期 Date of application:
经营单位 Executive company:	运输方式 Mode of transportation:	运输工具名称 Name of transportation tool:	提运单号 Delivery No.:
发货单位 Delivering company:	贸易方式 Mode of trade:	征免性质 Mode of tax levy:	结汇方式 Payment term:
许可证号 License No.:	运抵国(地区) Name of destination country (region):	指运港 Designated destination port:	境内货源地 Original place of delivered goods:
批准文号 No. of approved documents:	成交方式 Trade term:	运费 Freight:	保费 Insurance premium:	杂费 Additional expenses:
合同协议号 Contract No.:	件数 No. of packages:	包装种类 Type of package:	毛重(千克) Gross weight:	净重(千克) Net weight:
集装箱号 Container No.:	随附单证 Attached documents:		生产厂家 Manufacturer:	

标记唛码及备注
Marks, Nos and Remarks:

项号/商品编号/商品名称/规格型号/数量及单位/最终目的国(地区)/单价/总价/币制/征免
Item No. / Commodity code / Name of commodity / Specification / Quantity and unit / Final destination country (region) / Unit price / Total amount / Currency / Mode of tax levy

Continued

税费征收情况 Tax paid or not：			
录入员 Keyboarder： 录入单位 Record agency：	兹声明以上申报无讹并承担法律责任 We hereby claim the above declaration is true and we are reliable for all legal responsibilities.	海关审单批注及放行日期（签章） Customs examination comment and the approval date（seal）	
		审单 Document inspector：	审价 Price inspector：
报关员 Declarant：	申报单位（签章） Application entity（seal）	征税 Tax collector：	统计 Statistician：
单位地址 Address：		查验 Inspector：	放行 Approver：
邮编 Zip code： 电话 Tel：	填制日期 Date of application：		

Letter 2　Import Customs Declaration Form

中华人民共和国海关出口货物报关单
EXPORT CUSTOMS DECLARATION FORM OF THE PEOPLE'S REPUBLIC OF CHINA

预录入编号： No. of pre-record：				海关编号： No. of customs：
出口口岸 Port of export：	备案号 Record filing No.：	出口日期 Date of export：		申报日期 Date of application：
经营单位 Executive company：	运输方式 Mode of transportation：	运输工具名称 Name of transportation tool：		提运单号 Delivery No.：
发货单位 Delivering company：	贸易方式 Mode of trade/supervision：	征免性质 Mode of tax levy：		征税比例 Tax rate：
许可证号 License No.：	启运国（地区） Name of departure country（region）：	装货港 Port of loading：		境内目的地 Domestic destination：
批准文号 No. of approved documents：	成交方式 Trade term：	运费 Freight：	保费 Insurance premium：	杂费 Additional expenses：

Continued

合同协议号 Contract No.：	件数 No. of packages：	包装种类 Type of package：	毛重（千克） Gross weight：	净重（千克） Net weight：
集装箱号 Container No.：	随附单证 Attached documents：		用途 Usage：	
标记唛码及备注 Marks，Nos and Remarks：				

项号／商品编号／商品名称／规格型号／数量及单位／原产国（地区）／单价／总价／币制／征免
Item No. / Commodity code / Name of commodity / Specification / Quantity and unit / Country (region) of origin / Unit price / Total amount / Currency / Mode of tax levy

税费征收情况
Tax paid or not：

录入员 Keyboarder：	录入单位 Record agency：	兹声明以上申报无讹并承担法律责任 We hereby claim the above declaration is true and we are reliable for all legal responsibilities.	海关审单批注及放行日期（签章） Customs examination comment and the approval date（seal）	
			审单 Document inspector：	审价 Price inspector：
报关员 Declarant：		申报单位（签章） Application entity（seal）	征税 Tax collector：	统计 Statistician：
单位地址 Address：			查验 Inspector：	放行 Approver：
邮编 Zip code：	电话 Tel：	填制日期 Date of application：		

 Practical Usages

1. The Notes of the Beginning in Customs Declaration Form 报关单表头栏目的填报

1) No. of pre-record 预录入编号

It is given by the customs and formed automatically by the computer system when an exporter/importer is applying for customs declaration.
进出口货物申报时由海关计算机系统自动生成并打印的编号。

2) No. of customs 海关编号

   It is usually the same as No. of pre-record, automatically formed by the customs' computer system.

   通常海关编号同预录入编号,由计算机自行打印。

3) Port of import or export 进(出)口口岸

   Fill in the name and code of the customs where the goods actually enter or exit.

   填报货物实际进出境的口岸海关的名称及代码。

4) Record filing No. 备案号

   It refers to the number of the filed records approved by the customs, e.g. No. of Registration Manual.

   填报海关核发的准予备案的审批文件编号,如登记手册编号。

5) Date of export/import 进出口日期

   It refers to the date when cargoes enter into or exit from the customs territory.

   填报货物进出境的日期。

6) Date of application 申报日期

   Fill in the date when the customs accepts an importer/exporter's application for customs declaration.

   填报海关接收进出口商进出境申报的日期。

7) Executive company 经营单位

   Fill in the Chinese name and customs registration code of the company who signs and executes the import or export contract.

   填报海关注册登记的对外签订并执行进出口贸易合同的单位中文名称及海关注册编码。

8) Mode of transportation 运输方式

   Fill in the name or code of transporting mode by which the goods finally enter or exit or that of the goods' flow category in the customs territory.

   根据货物实际进出境的运输方式或货物在境内流向的类别,选择填报相应的运输方式名称或代码,见表10-1。

表 10-1 部分运输方式代码表及说明

代码	名称	运输方式说明
1	监管仓库(supervised warehouse)	境内存入出口监管仓库和出口监管仓库退仓
2	水路运输(waterway transport)	
3	铁路运输(railway transport)	

续表

代码	名称	运输方式说明
4	公路运输(roadway transport)	
5	航空运输(airway transport)	

9) Name of transportation tool 运输工具名称

   Fill in the name and number of transportation tool.

   填报载运货物进出境的运输工具名称及运输工具编号。

10) Delivery No. 提运单号

    Fill in the number of transportation document, e.g. Ocean Bill of Lading.

    填报进出口货物提单或运单编号,如海运提单号。

11) Receiving company/Delivering company 收货单位/发货单位

    Receiving company refers to the end customer or user of the imported goods. Delivering company refers to the domestic producer or seller of the exported goods. Fill in the Chinese name and registration code of the relevant company.

    收货单位指进口货物在境内的最终消费或使用单位;发货单位指出口货物在境内的生产或销售单位。填报相关单位的中文名称及编码。

12) Mode of trade/supervision 贸易方式(监管方式)

    Fill in the abbreviation and code of the customs mode of trade/supervision

    根据海关规定的"贸易方式(监管方式)代码表"填报贸易(监管)方式简称及代码。

13) Mode of tax levy 征免性质

    Fill in the abbreviation or code of customs tax levy.

    根据海关规定的"征免性质代码表"填报征免性质简称或代码。

14) Tax rate/Payment term 征税比例/结汇方式

    Tax rate is free for filling in import declaration. Payment term should be filled in the abbreviation or code of customs payment term.

    进口报关单征税比例栏目免予填报。出口报关单按海关规定的"结汇方式代码表"(见表10-2)选择填报相应的结汇方式名称或代码。

表10-2 部分结汇方式代码表

代码	简称	英文缩写	英文名称
1	信汇	M/T	Mail Transfer
2	电汇	T/T	Telegraphic Transfer
3	票汇	D/D	Remittance by Banker's Demand Draft

续表

代码	简称	英文缩写	英文名称
4	付款交单	D/P	Documents against Payment
5	承兑交单	D/A	Documents against Acceptance
6	信用证	L/C	Letter of Credit

15) License No. 许可证号

　　Fill in the license number.

　　填写进出口货物许可证号。

16) Name of departure country(region)/Name of destination country (region) 启运国(地区)/运抵国(地区)

　　Name of departure country (region) refers to the country (region) the goods departed from; Name of destination country (region) refers to the final destination the goods will reach. In transshipment, if there is some transaction occurring, fill in the name or code of transshipment country (region).

　　启运国/地区填报进口货物启始发出并直接运抵我国的国家/地区名称或代码。运抵国/地区填报出口货物离开我国关境直接运抵的国家/地区名称或代码。经第三国/地区中转(转运)的货物,在运输中转国/地区发生任何商业性交易的情况下,填报中转国/地区名称或代码。

17) Port of loading /Designated destination port 装货港/指运港

　　Port of loading refers to the final port where the goods are loaded. Designated destination port refers to the final destination port.

　　装货港填报进口货物在运抵我国关境前的最后一个境外装运港。指运港填报出口货物运往境外的最终目的港。

18) Domestic destination/Original place of delivered goods 境内目的地/境内货源地

　　Domestic destination refers to final destination in China. Original place of delivered goods refers to the place where the goods originally produced or delivered.

　　境内目的地填报已知的进口货物在我国关境内的最终运抵地。境内货源地填报出口货物在我国关境内的生产地或原始发货地。

19) No. of approved documents 批准文号

　　Fill in the approved documents and numbers except for import/export license.

　　填写除进出口货物许可证外的其他批准文件及编号。

20）Trade term 成交方式

Fill in the trade term listed in commercial invoice，such as FOB，CIF，CFR.

填报进出口货物商业发票中价格成交方式，如 FOB，CIF，CFR 等海关申报代码，如表 10-3 所示。

表 10-3　成交方式代码表

成交方式代码	成交方式名称	成交方式代码	成交方式名称
1	CIF	4	C&I
2	CFR(C&F/CNF)	5	市场价
3	FOB	6	垫仓

21）Freight 运费

Fill in the freight incurred before the goods are unloaded in China or after the goods are loaded for delivery.

填报进口货物运抵我国境内输入地点起卸前的运输费用，出口货物运至我国境内输出地点装载后的运输费用。（注：可按"运费率/1""币种代码/运费单价/2""币种代码/运费总价/3"三选一填报。）

22）Insurance premium 保费

Fill in the premium incurred before the goods are unloaded in China or after the goods are loaded for delivery.

填报进口货物运抵我国境内输入地点起卸前的保险费用，出口货物运至我国境内输出地点装载后的保险费用。（注：可按"保险费率/1""币种代码/保险总价/3"二选一填报。）

23）Additional expenses 杂费

The expenses incurred during transaction and should be included in or deducted from the customs value of goods

填报成交价格以外的、应计入完税价格或从完税价格中扣除的费用。

24）Contract No. 合同协议号

25）Number of packages 件数

Fill in the number of packages. If the goods are in bulk or nude, fill in "1".

填报有外包装的进出口货物的总件数。散装、裸装货物填报"1"。

26）Type of package 包装种类

Fill in carton, bale, drum, case, etc. according to the type of goods' package.

根据货物包装情况，填写纸板箱、包、桶、箱等。

27) Gross weight 毛重

It refers to the goods weight with package. The unit is kilogram. If the weight is less than one kilogram, fill in "1".

填报进出口货物及其包装材料的重量之和。计量单位为千克,不足1千克的填报为"1"。

28) Net weight 净重

It refers to the goods weight without package. The unit is kilogram. If the weight is less than one kilogram, fill in "1".

填报进出口货物的毛重减去外包装材料后的重量。计量单位为千克,不足1千克的填报为"1"。

29) Container No. 集装箱号

The form is "container No. /specification/weight".

填报格式为:集装箱号/集装箱规格/集装箱自重。

30) Attached documents 随附单据

Fill in the No. of the necessary documents attached to the declaration form.

随附单证是指随进出口货物报关单一并向海关递交的,除商业和货运单证及进出口许可证以外的监管证件。

31) Usage/Manufacturer 用途/生产厂家

Fill in the actual usage of imported goods/ the manufacturer of exported goods.

填写进口货物境内的实际用途名称或代码/出口货物境内生产企业的名称。

32) Marks, Nos and remarks 标记唛码及备注

Fill in the shipping marks and the additional matters to be stated.

填报运输标记及需要补充或特别说明的事项。

2. The Notes of the Body in Customs Declaration Form 报关单表体栏目的填报

1) Item No. and commodity code 项号和商品编号

Item No. refers to the serial number of the goods in customs declaration form. Commodity code consists of 10 figures. The former 8 figures are made out according to the Commodity Classification for China Customs Statistics and the latter 2 is additional code made by the customs.

项号是指货物在本报关单中的商品顺序编号。商品编号共10位数字,前8位为根据"中华人民共和国海关统计商品目录"确定的商品编码,后2位为海关附加编号。

2) The name of commodity and specification 商品名称、规格型号

Fill in the name of commodity in the first line and specification in the second line.

第一行填报进出口货物商品名称,第二行填报规格型号。

3) Quantity and unit 数量及单位

In the first line fill in the quantity and the first legal unit for measurement; in the second line fill in the quantity and the second legal unit for measurement; in the third line fill in the quantity and the unit for measurement in transaction.

本栏分三行填报。

(1) 第一行填报数量及第一法定计量单位。

(2) 第二行填报数量及第二法定计量单位。无法定第二计量单位的,第二行为空。

(3) 第三行填报数量及成交计量单位。成交计量单位与法定计量单位一致时,第三行为空。

4) Country(region) of origin/Final destination country（region）原产国(地区)/最终目的国(地区)

Fill in the country（region）where imported goods were originally produced, explored or processed/the country（region）where exported goods will be finally consumed, used or processed.

原产地国(地区)是指进口货物的生产、开采或加工制造的国家或地区。最终目的国(地区)是指已知的出口货物被最终实际消费、使用或作进一步加工制造的国家或地区。

5) Unit price and total amount 单价和总价

6) Currency 币制

Fill in the currency name or code according to the customs code of currency.

按照海关规定的"货币代码表"(见表10-4)选择填报相应的货币名称或代码。

表 10-4　部分货币代码表

货币代码	货币符号	货币名称	货币代码	货币符号	货币名称
110	HKD	港币	116	JPY	日本元
142	CNY	人民币	303	GBP	英镑
502	USD	美元	300	EUR	欧元

7) Mode of tax levy 征免

Fill in the name or code in the customs code of tax levy, reduction or exemption.

根据海关规定的"征减免税方式代码表"填报相应的名称或代码。

8) Tax paid or not 税费征收情况

It is filled by the customs officer.

此栏由海关工作人员填制。

9) Application entity (seal) 申报单位(签章)

Sign with seal. The seal is specially used only for customs.

签字盖章。此章为海关专用章。

Problems Solving

1. Discuss with your partners about the differences between import customs declaration form and export customs declaration form.
2. The following is an introduction to a customs clearance agent. Fill in the blanks with the words given below.

| cartons | addition | delivery | offering | range |

Our company is a true customs clearance agent, (1) _____ a one stop solution for any customs clearance requirements an importer may have. In (2) _____ to being your customs clearance agent, we can also provide a full (3) _____ of haulage solutions, whether you are moving (4) _____, pallets or containers. Thanks to strong working relationships with our selected network of partners, we can achieve prompt (5) _____ of your cargo once customs clearance has been completed.

Section 4 Skills Training and Case Study Samples

Skills Training

A. There are ten incomplete sentences in this part. For each sentence there are three choices marked A, B and C. Choose the one that best completes the sentence.

1. If the goods are delivered in bulk or nude, the column of No. of packages in the customs declaration form should be filled in _____.

  A. 0   B. blank   C. 1

2. If the net weight of the goods is 0.5 kilogram, the column of Net weight in the customs declaration form should be filled in _____.

  A. 0.5   B. 1.5   C. 1

3. If container No. is TEXU4806541, container's specification is 20 feet, and container's weight is 2365 kilogram. The column of Container No. in the customs declaration form should be _____.

  A. TEXU4806541/20/2365　　　　　　B. TEXU4806541
  C. TEXU4806541/2365

4. The column of Quantity and unit in the customs declaration form should be fill in _____ lines.
  A. 1　　　　　　B. 2　　　　　　C. 3

5. Commodity code in the customs declaration form consists of _____ figures.
  A. 8　　　　　　B. 10　　　　　C. 9

6. The enterprises shall apply China E-Port _____ and directly declare to the customs.
  A. platform　　　B. station　　　C. location

7. The enterprises shall input all customs _____ once only.
  A. information　　B. data　　　　C. details

8. Customs shall establish a special window to _____ customs clearance.
  A. increase　　　B. improve　　　C. facilitate

9. Without relevant documents, customs are unable to identify the goods classification and the _____ of goods value.
  A. assessment　　B. concession　　C. confirmation

10. In the case that the description, the specifications and the quantity of the goods are determinate, the enterprises can _____ to the customs in advance.
  A. release　　　B. declare　　　C. demand

B. Translate the following terms into English.

报关　　　　　　　　检验
进口许可证　　　　　电子口岸平台
原产地　　　　　　　监管
审单　　　　　　　　估价
主管地海关　　　　　电子回执

C. Translate the following sentences into Chinese.

1. An export license shall be subject to the "one license for one customs".
2. A Certificate of Origin is required by the customs as one of the key bases for applying tariff rates.
3. Customs is an agency of the government responsible for checking all import goods and assessing and collecting duties.
4. In Chinese mainland, import and export declarations must be lodged before cargoes are released.

5. An inspection and quarantine report agency shall abide by the relevant laws and regulations on entry-exit inspection and quarantine.

Case Study Samples

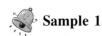 **Sample 1**

Import Customs Declaration

BTL Industry Co., Ltd. is a professional and experienced prototype company which plans to import some machines for their production in a project encouraged by local government. The machines to be imported are in the scope of the goods with duty reduction or exemption. Before making import customs declaration, the company needs to go through the following procedures:

(1) File an application to the customs for the approval of tax reduction or exemption;

(2) Prepare the following documents required by the customs:
- business license;
- import and export contract;
- the documents of approval from the competent commerce department;
- articles of association.

(3) The customs conduct examination to the application of the company;

(4) If there is nothing wrong, the customs complete the work of registration and archival filing, and issue the "tax reduction or exemption certificate" to the company;

(5) After obtaining the "tax reduction or exemption certificate", the company started to make import customs declaration.

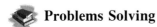 **Problems Solving**

1. If your company wants to import some goods, what documents may be required in import customs declaration?
2. Do you know what kinds of import/export goods must go through the procedures mentioned in the passage?

 Sample 2

Export Declaration

Nanjing Yunda Import & Export Co., Ltd. is a joint venture producing all kinds of

Suction Fans with the materials from the domestic market. In May, 2024, Nanjing Yunda Import & Export Co., Ltd. entrusted ABC International Freight Forwarding Co., Ltd. to lodge the export declaration in Shanghai Pudong customs (customs code: 2210). Customs registration code of Nanjing Yunda Import & Export Co., Ltd. is 311893 xxxx. The freight rate is 5%.

Problems Solving

1. If you are required to lodge an export customs declaration for the above goods, what documents should you prepare for the customs declaration?
2. Please refer to the Commercial Invoice and Packing List in Unit 7 Documents and make out an export customs declaration form.

Section 5 Elevating Vision and Useful Expressions

> Elevating Vision

China Customs Organizations, Functions and Tasks

China Customs is a state organ responsible for the supervision and control over means of transport, goods, luggage, postal items and other articles entering or leaving China's territory, the collection of Customs duties, taxes and fees, the prevention of smuggling, the compilation of the Customs statistics and dealing with other Customs matters.

Shortly after the founding of the People's Republic of China, the Customs General Administration was set up by the State Council (Oct. 25, 1949). Located in Beijing, the Customs General Administration now mainly consists of altogether 12 departments and offices, i. e. General Office; Department of Policy and Legal Affairs; Department of Supervision; Department of Duty Collection; Department of Processing Trade Management; Department of Statistics; Department of Scientific and Technological Development; Bureau of Investigation; Anti-smuggling Criminal Investigation Bureau; Department of Human Resources Management; Department of Finance and Equipment; Department of International Cooperation.

The main task of the Customs General Administration of the People's Republic of China is, under the leadership of the State Council, to lead and organize Customs offices throughout the country in the enforcement of the "Customs Law" and related state policies and regulations, and in the promotion and protection of socialist modernization.

Considering there are so many Customs offices and its heavy workload in Guangdong Province, the Customs General Administration has set up its sub-office in Guangzhou to assist it in administering the Customs offices in the province. This sub-office is named Guangdong Regional Customs Office.

The main functions of the Customs General Administration shall be stated as the followings:

(1) To draft and enact the policies and principles on Customs work; to participate in drawing up and amending the Customs Import and Export Tariff; to enact other statutes on Customs operation; and to inspect, supervise and direct the enforcement of them by the Customs offices throughout the country;

(2) To participate in drafting international treaties and agreements on Customs affairs;

(3) To conduct the unified handling of tariff reductions and exemptions;

(4) To organize and guide the preventive work of the Customs offices throughout the country;

(5) To examine applications for reviewing disputes on duty payments and applications for reviewing Customs decisions on penalties;

(6) To compile Customs statistics;

(7) To administer organizations, staffing, vocational training and appointments and removals of directors of Customs Offices throughout the country; and to exercise leadership in Customs schools and colleges;

(8) To organize the work of research and development, introduction and management of Customs technological facilities;

(9) To administer audit and supervise all Customs financial affairs, equipment, fixed assets and capital construction;

(10) To strengthen ties and co-operation and external exchanges with overseas Customs Services, international Customs organizations and other international

organizations concerned.

 Useful Expression

报 关 用 语	
air waybill 航空运单	import license 进口许可证
bonded warehouse 保税仓库	inspection certificate of quality 品质检验证书
booking list 定舱清单	inspection certificate of weight 重量检验证书
cargo in bulk 散装货	landing charges 卸货费
cargo in nude 裸装货	optional charges 选港费
cargo insurance 货物运输保险	optional port 选择港
cargo receipt 货物收据	original B/L 正本提单
certificate of origin 产地证明书	port dues 港务费
certificate of quality 货物品质证书	purchase confirmation 购货确认书
certificate of quantity 货物数量证明书	purchase contract 购货合同
clean bill of lading 清洁提单	sales confirmation 销售确认书
commission 佣金	sales contract 销售合同
commodity code 商品编码	shipment advice 装运通知
commodity inspection and quarantine bureau(CIQ) 商品检验检疫局	shipping liner 班轮
	shipping space 舱位
compensation trade 补偿贸易	take delivery of goods 提货
conditions of carriage 货运条件	time charter 定期租船
consignor 托运人	time of delivery 交货时间
consignee 收货人	time of shipment 装运期限
customs clearance 报关/清关	trade term 贸易术语
export license 出口许可证	voyage charter 程租船
discharge 卸货	
freight 运费	

Unit 11

Account Settlement

Learning Objectives

- To know the methods of payment in freight forwarding services
- To know the advantages and disadvantages of basic methods of payment
- To learn the key words and expressions in account settlement

Skill Developing Objectives

- To develop communication skills in account settlement
- To develop writing skills in account settlement

Section 1　Theme Lead-in

Read the following passage to get a better understanding of this unit.

Payment

A payment is the transfer of money from one party (such as a person or company) to another. It is usually made in exchange for the provision of goods, services or both, or to fulfill a legal obligation. The simplest and oldest form of payment is barter, the exchange of one good or service for another. In the modern world, common means of payment include money, cheque, letter of credit, or bank transfer. And in trade such payments are frequently preceded by an invoice or result in a receipt.

Pay cash

The buyer shall pay the money to the seller through bank, after the contract is signed or the order is made, or within the time specified by the agreement. Under other conditions, the buyer shall pay the money before the shipment, taking it as a condition for the seller. So this method is most advantageous to the seller, but the buyer will take the bigger risk. Actually, the method is just used for special processing, or the buyer is eager to buy the best-selling goods.

Remittance

Remittance is a process that the payer instructs his bank or other institutions to have a payment made to the payee. Four parties are involved in the remittance business: remitter, the payee, the remitting bank and the paying bank. Remittance can be made by mail, telegraph and draft.

Telegraphic Transfer (T/T)

Telegraphic Transfer (T/T) is a process that the remitting bank, at the request of the remittance, sends a cable to its correspondent bank in the country concerned instruction it to make a certain amount of payment to payee. The payee can receive payment promptly, but the charges for this type of transfer are relatively high.

Collection

Collection is a process through which the global banking system acts on behalf of an exporter (or seller) to collect each payment or a time draft from the importer (or buyer) in return for documents required for taking delivery of the ordered goods.

Documentary collection means collection of financial documents and commercial documents. There are Documents against Payment (D/P) and Documents against

Acceptance (D/A). Under D/P, the exporter releases the documents on the condition that the importer has made the payment. Under D/A, the exporter release the documents on the condition that the importer has made acceptance on the draft.

Cash on delivery

This is a kind of principle. The buyer shall pay the money upon receiving the goods from the seller, as there are no other requirements. The method "payment on delivery" usually refers to cash payment on delivery. It is usually used in the situation of physical delivery, like EXW Contract.

Payment by L/C

Being the most commonly used method in international trade, it is a conditional promise of payment made by the bank. At the request of the importer, the bank issues the L/C within a certain period of time. It states that the bank will pay a specified sum of money to a beneficiary, normally the exporter, on presentation of particular documents.

In law, the payer is the party making a payment while the payee is the party receiving the payment. Payments may be classified by the number of parties involved to consummate a transaction. For example, a credit card transaction in the United States requires a minimum of four parties (the purchaser, the seller, the issuing bank, and the acquiring bank). A cash payment requires a minimum of three parties (the seller, the purchaser, and the issuer of the currency). A barter payment requires a minimum of two parties (the purchaser and the seller).

 Notes

1. A payment is the transfer of money from one party (such as a person or company) to another.
   支付指的是金钱从一方(比如某个人或某个公司)转移至另一方。

2. In the modern world, common means of payment include cash, cheque, letter of credit, or bank transfer.
   在当代社会,常见的支付手段包括现金、支票、信用证以及银行转账。

3. The buyer shall pay the money to the seller through bank, after the contract is signed or the order is made, or within the time specified by the agreement.
   一旦订立合同或是订单成立,或在协议规定的时间范围内,买方应通过银行将钱款付给卖方。

4. Under other conditions, the buyer shall pay the money before the shipment,

taking it as a condition for the seller.
在其他情况下,应卖方的要求,买方也会在货物装运之前付款。

5. The buyer shall pay the money upon receiving the goods from the seller, as there are no other requirements.
如果没有其他要求,买方会在收到货物的时候付款给卖方。

6. Remittance is a process that the payer instructs his bank or other institutions to have a payment made to the payee.
汇付是指付款人通过银行或其他途径将款项汇交收款人。

7. Telegraphic Transfer (T/T) is a process that the remitting bank, at the request of the remittance, sends a cable to its correspondent bank in the country concerned instruction it to make a certain amount of payment to payee.
电汇是汇出行应汇款人的申请,电报通知另一国家的代理行指示解付一定金额给收款人的一种汇款方式。

8. Collection is a process through which the global banking system acts on behalf of an exporter (or seller) to collect each payment or a time draft from the importer (or buyer) in return for documents required for taking delivery of the ordered goods.
托收是全球银行系统代表出口商(卖方)向进口商(买方)收取货款或远期汇票,并交付提取订单货物所需单据的一种过程。

9. Under D/P, the exporter releases the documents on the condition that the importer has made the payment. Under D/A, the exporter release the documents on the condition that the importer has made acceptance on the draft.
付款交单是指出口人的交单是以进口人的付款为条件;承兑交单是指出口人的交单以进口人在汇票上承兑为条件。

10. The method "payment on delivery" usually refers to cash payment on delivery. It is usually used in the situation of physical delivery, like EXW Contract.
交货付款的方式通常指的是交货付现金。它通常应用于像工厂交货合同这种类型的实物交收。

11. At the request of the importer, the bank issues the L/C within a certain period of time.
应进口商的要求,银行在一定期限内开立信用证。

12. It states that the bank will pay a specified sum of money to a beneficiary, normally the exporter, on presentation of particular documents.
信用证规定银行应在出口商提示特定的单据时,向受益人支付规定的款项。

13. Payments may be classified by the number of parties involved to consummate a transaction.

    由于完成交易牵涉的各方参与,付款方式可以进行多种分类。

14. A credit card transaction in the United States requires a minimum of four parties: (the purchaser, the seller, the issuing bank, and the acquiring bank).

    在美国,信用卡付款交易至少需要四方当事人:买方、卖方、开证银行和通知行。

15. A cash payment requires a minimum of three parties (the seller, the purchaser, and the issuer of the currency).

    现金支付至少需要三方当事人:卖方、买方和货币发行人。

16. A barter payment requires a minimum of two parties (the purchaser and the seller).

    易货支付至少需要两方当事人:买方和卖方。

 Problems Solving

1. What payment methods are mentioned in the passage? And which one do you think is the safest? Why?

2. Decide whether the following statement is true or false according to the passage?

（1）Under D/A, the exporter releases the documents on the condition that the importer has made the payment.　　　　　　　　　　　　　　　　　　　　（　）

（2）A credit card transaction requires a minimum of three parties: the purchaser, the seller, and the issuing bank.　　　　　　　　　　　　　　　　　　　　（　）

（3）COD usually refers to payment on delivery.　　　　　　　　　　　（　）

（4）A barter payment requires a minimum of two parties: the purchaser and the seller.　　　　　　　　　　　　　　　　　　　　　　　　　　　　　　　　　（　）

（5）Remittance is a process that the payer instructs his bank or other institutions to have a payment made to the payee.　　　　　　　　　　　　　　　　　　　（　）

 # Section 2　Conversations and Warm-up

┌─ **Conversations** ─┐

 Conversation 1　Terms of Payment

(A is an accountant with a trading company, who is talking with B, Mr. Smith, a sales manager in a freight forwarding company.)

A: Good morning, Mr. Smith. I'd like to talk about the payment for your freight forwarding services.

B: Okay. We usually accept pay my hent against documents.

A: What does it mean?

B: It means the relevant documents can only be handed over when you have paid the amount on the draft.

A: Oh. I see. Do you accept other methods?

B: We also accept deposit deduction.

A: Can you explain it in detail?

B: Sure. It means the charge will be deducted from your deposit account, on condition that you have enough money in your account.

A: Thank you for your information.

 Conversation 2   Accounts Settlement

(*A is an exporter, who is talking with B, Mr. Wang, a sales manager of a freight forwarding company.*)

A: Well, we've settled the question of price, quality and quantity. Now what about the terms of payment?

B: Our normal payment term is 30 days.

A: Do you mean monthly statement?

B: Yes. Monthly statement will be provided before the 5th of each month for all the accounts of the preceding month.

A: I see. Could we pay in CNY?

B: Yes. The currency of payment shall be CNY or USD and payment shall be made via telegraphic transfer to our nominated bank account.

A: Okay. Please send me your beneficiary bank name and address, bank code, swift code and account number.

B: Sure. I will email you the details soon.

 Conversation 3   Bargaining for Agent Payment

(*A is Mr. Brown, a sales manager in a freight forwarding company, who is talking with B, Ms. Lily, an exporter.*)

A: Good morning, Ms. Lily.

B: Good morning, Mr. Brown.

A: Have you got our offer?

B: Yes, but we're sorry to tell you that your collected freight is far beyond our expectation and it is difficult for us to accept it. Could you reduce the price by 10%?

A: 10%? You can't be serious. As mentioned in our previous letter, our collected freight has been carefully calculated and cut to the limit.

B: Well, if you stick to it, the collected freight will leave us no profit. To meet each other half way, what do you say to payment by installment?

A: Considering our good business relations in the past, we agree to your proposal of payments by installment. Please remit the 10% down payment to us by T/T and payment of the balance is to be covered over five equal installments.

B: Couldn't be better. We agree that the payment can be divided into five installments. Thank you very much for your consideration.

A: My pleasure. Looking forward to receiving you order as soon as possible.

 Warm-up

A. Match the definitions in Column B with the terms in Column A.

A	B
1. deposit	A. a conditional promise of payment made by a bank
2. cash on delivery	B. a partial payment made at the time of purchase
3. endorse	C. a type of transaction in which payment for a good is made at the time of delivery
4. letter of credit	D. a check paid by a bank to another bank or to a particular person or organization
5. bank draft	E. to designate oneself as payee of a check or other document by signing, usually on the reverse side of the instrument

B. The following is a passage about the installment. Fill in the blanks with the words given in the box and discuss with your partners about the roles that an installment plays in business activities.

| interest | amount | monetary | rate | repayment |

An installment payment is a (1) _____ payment made on a loan that has been disbursed. It is a periodic payment that is typically of a predetermined amount that includes a percentage of (2) _____ as well as a percentage of principal. There is the potential for the (3) _____ of an installment payment to vary if the loan itself has a variable interest (4) _____. An installment payment is a common type of

(5) _____ plan for many loans.

C. Make up a dialogue according to the following situation.

Student A works as an accountant with a freight forwarding company, and Student B is a client who wants to know the details about account settlement for freight forwarding services. Student A and Student B will act out the dialogue about account settlement in freight services.

The dialogue should cover the following information: greetings, the methods of account settlement, and bargaining for different methods of payment.

Section 3　Format Writings and Practical Usages

⁺–⁺–⁺–⁺–⁺–⁺–⁺–⁺–⁺
｜ Format Writings ｜
⁺–⁺–⁺–⁺–⁺–⁺–⁺–⁺–⁺

After reading the following passage, you are required to discuss with your partners and to complete the statements that follow the questions.

Bill of Exchange

A bill of exchange or "draft" is a written order by the drawer to the drawee to pay money to the payee. It is essentially an order made by one person to another to pay money to a third person.

A common type of bill of exchange is the cheque (check in American English), as a bill of exchange drawn on a banker and payable on demand. Bills of exchange are used primarily in international trade, and are written orders by one person to his bank to pay the bearer a specific sum on a specific date.

A bill of exchange requires three parties—the drawer, the drawee, and the payee. The person who draws the bill is called the drawer. He gives the order to pay money to the third party. The party upon whom the bill is drawn is called the drawee. He is the person to whom the bill is addressed and who is ordered to pay. He becomes an acceptor when he indicates his willingness to pay the bill. The party in whose favor the bill is drawn or is payable is called the payee. The parties need not all be distinct persons. Thus, the drawer may draw on himself payable to his own order.

A bill of exchange may be endorsed by the payee in favor of a third party, who may in turn endorse it to a fourth, and so on indefinitely. The "holder in due course" may claim the amount of the bill against the drawee and all previous endorsers, regardless of any counterclaims that may have disabled the previous payee or endorser from doing so. This is what is meant by saying that a bill is negotiable.

 Problems Solving

1. What is a bill of exchange?
2. What is a common type of bill of exchange?
3. How many parties are required in a bill of exchange?
4. Can a bill of exchange be endorsed?
5. Could the "holder in due course" claim the amount of the bill against the drawer?

 Writing Samples

Letter 1   Account Settlement

April 15, 2024

Dear Mrs. Yeo,

　　Your e-mail of April 14 was duly received, and we hand you herewith a statement of your account as requested, which we hope you will find correct.

　　We would like to remind you that because your outstanding on credit has piled up to a recognized level and the payment for this single ocean freight shipment is over US $5,000, immediate remittance is required. The payment shall be made in CNY and via telegraphic transfer to our nominated bank account.

　　We look forward receiving your cheque by return.

Yours sincerely,

Letter 2   Payment Demand

April 25, 2024

Dear Mrs. Yeo,

　　Further to our letter of April 15 in which we requested that you pay the outstanding sum of US $5,800 to our account, we were disappointed to discover yesterday that we have still not received a cheque from you for the overdue amount.

　　We understand that it is sometimes difficult to meet our debts. If you are experiencing difficulties with our repayment scheme, please come to our company to discuss the matter. We assure you that we shall adopt a very understanding attitude. We look forward to hearing from you within the next week.

Yours sincerely,

 Practical Usages

1. Account Settlement 结算

- We would like to remind you that because your outstanding on credit has piled up to a recognized level and the payment for this single ocean freight shipment is over US＄5,000, immediate remittance is required.
  我们想提醒您,由于您的未偿信用已很可观,而且这笔货运账款超过5000美元,因此,需要您即时支付。

- The payment shall be made in CNY and via telegraphic transfer to our nominated bank account.
  付款货币为人民币,通过电汇方式转账到我方指定账户。

2. Payment Demand 催款

- Further to our letter of April 15 in which we requested that you pay the outstanding sum of US＄5,800 to our account, we were disappointed to discover yesterday that we have still not received a cheque from you for the overdue amount.
  我方曾于4月15日去函要求您将总额为5,800美元的未结账款汇入我方账户。但到昨天为止,仍未收到您的支票,对此我们深感失望。

- According to our records, the sum of HK＄5,800 was due on March 15 2024.
  根据我方记录,贵方所欠账款共计5,800港元,已于2024年3月15日到期。

- In the light of your present financial difficulties, we are prepared to accept an immediate payment of HK＄5,800 with the balance being settled over the next.
  鉴于贵方目前的财务困境,我们拟要求贵方即时支付5,800港元,余额于下两个月内结清。

- If you are unable to settle your account by the end of next week, I am afraid we will be forced to pass the matter over to our legal department.
  贵方若在下周结束之前不能结清账款,我们恐怕只能将此事提交本公司法律部处理。

Problems Solving

1. The following is a letter for payment demand. Please fill in the blanks with the words given below.

| repayments | sum | outstanding | unfortunate | limit |

Dear Sir,

I have recently sent you a letter regarding the (1) _____ balance of your account with our company. According to our records, you have failed to make any (2) _____ whatsoever and the (3) _____ of US＄4,500 is now overdue.

We certainly would not like to reduce your credit (4) _____ for future purchases. I urge you in the strongest terms, therefore, to contact me within the next seven days so that this (5) _____ situation can be sorted out.

I look forward to hearing from you within the next week.

Yours faithfully,

2. Suppose your client doesn't make his repayment. Write a letter for payment demand.

Section 4 Skills Training and Case Study Samples

Skills Training

A. There are ten incomplete sentences in this part. For each sentence there are three choices marked A, B and C. Choose the one that best completes the sentence.

1. Please remit the 5% down payment to us by T/T and payment of the balance is to be covered over three equal _____.

    A. installments   B. acceptance   C. amount

2. A bill of exchange may be _____ by the payee in favor of a third party.

    A. offered   B. endorsed   C. accepted

3. We have received your letter of April 15 in which you requested that we pay the _____ sum of US＄5,800 to your account.

    A. announcing   B. demanding   C. outstanding

4. We have not received a cheque from you for the _____ amount.

    A. overdue   B. available   C. durable

5. T/T is a process that the _____ bank sends a cable to its correspondent bank

to make a certain amount of payment to payee.

    A. committing   B. remitting   C. admitting

6. Under D/P, the exporter _____ the documents on the condition that the importer has made the payment.

    A. releases   B. prepares   C. accepts

7. At the request of the importer, the bank _____ the L/C within a certain period of time.

    A. establishes   B. draws   C. issues

8. A payment is the _____ of money from one party (such as a person or company) to another.

    A. transfer   B. borrowing   C. credit

9. The simplest and oldest form of payment is _____, the exchange of one good or service for another.

    A. agent   B. exhibition   C. barter

10. In real trade situation, payments are frequently preceded by an invoice or result in a _____.

    A. report   B. invoice   C. receipt

B. Translate the following terms into English.

分期付款   电汇
备用金扣款   付款交单
承兑交单   应付账款
支票   余额
开户银行   账号

C. Translate the following sentences into Chinese.

1. You'd better take enough cash, in case they don't accept credit cards.
2. With a bank's involvement, the freight forwarder no longer needs to reply on the willingness and capability of the buyer to make payment.
3. The invoice value may exceed the credit, that is to say, the freight forwarder has shipped a larger quantity of goods than is permitted.
4. You still have not cleared your balance of HK $3,000, which is now 30 days overdue.
5. We look forward to receiving your cheque in full settlement of your overdue account within the next three day.

Case Study Samples

Sample 1

How to Write a Sample Payment Agreement

Basic Information

Please note that any business agreement should include basic identifying information. In the introductory section of the payment agreement, it includes:
- The full legal name of the person who will make the payment;
- The full legal name of the person who will receive the payment;
- The date the agreement goes into effect.

Services and Payment Terms

Write, in detail, what services and goods you're responsible for and the payments the other party is liable for. The body of payment should include information like:
- A description of what services and goods will be rendered.
- Payment amount or rate: Note if the payment is a fixed fee, or if it will be an hourly rate. If work is paid on an hourly basis, record the hourly rate and any cap on hours for the project.
- Payment Schedule: For example, you may receive payments on a monthly basis, or you may receive the entire balance when the work is complete. List exact dates timelines and conditions of payment.
- Payment method: Detail whether payments can be made by check, credit.card, cash or bank transfer.
- Explain your policy on late fees or interest charges if payments aren't made on time.

If the project involves any expenses, note what the common expenses are and which party is responsible for them.

Problems Solving

1. What elements should be included in a sample payment agreement? Make a three-minute presentation to introduce how to write a sample payment agreement. You can use some visual aid to help you to express yourself, such as a flowchart, a diagram or a PPT.

2. What payment method will you choose to make the payment for freight forwarding services? Why?

3. Suppose you are a freight forwarder. Write a payment agreement to your client.

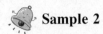 **Sample 2**

Installment Payment Agreement

April 25, 2024

Dear Mr. Reeve,

Re: Installment Payment Agreement

This is to confirm the arrangement under which we will accept payment of our outstanding account of HK＄3,000 in installments. You will sign and return the enclosed copy of this letter indicating admission of the full amount of the account and acceptance of the terms of our agreement.

We will, then, accept payment of the account, together with interest at the rate of 3％ per month, in consecutive, monthly installments of HK＄1,000, commencing May 15 and continuing on the June 15 of each successive month until paid off in full. Time will be considered to be of the essence of this arrangement. Each payment will be applied: first, to accrued interest and, second, to principal.

If there is default in making any payment, at our option, the full balance owing on the account, together with accrued agreed interest, shall immediately become due and payable and continue to accrue interest, before and after judgment, at the same rate of interest until paid off in full.

Please return the signed copy of this agreement with your first payment before the commencement dates of the monthly installments otherwise this agreement is null and void.

Sincerely,

Ho Yuen

Problems Solving

1. What is installment payment? Could you tell the reason why an installment payment is commonly used in business activities?
2. Suppose you are experiencing the difficulties with your debts. Write a letter to your freight forwarder, requesting for the change in payment terms from payment against document to installment payment.

Section 5　Elevating Vision and Useful Expressions

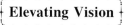

Letter of Credit

A letter of credit, abbreviated as L/C, is a document issued by a financial institution, or a similar party, assuring payment to a seller of goods and/or services provided certain documents have been presented to the bank.

These are documents that prove that the seller has performed the duties under an underlying contract (e. g., sale of goods contract) and the goods (or services) have been supplied as agreed. In return for these documents, the beneficiary receives payment from the financial institution that issued the letter of credit.

The letter of credit is often used in international transactions to ensure that payment will be received where the buyer and seller may not know each other and are operating in different countries. It is regarded as the most reliable method of payment, as it serves as a guarantee to the seller that it will be paid regardless of whether the buyer ultimately fails to pay. In this way, the risk that the buyer will fail to pay is transferred from the seller to the letter of credit's issuer. The letter of credit can also be used to ensure that all the agreed upon standards and quality of goods are met by the supplier, provided that these requirements are reflected in the documents described in the letter of credit.

One of the primary peculiarities of the documentary credit is that the payment obligation is independent from the underlying contract of sale or any other contract in the transaction. Thus the bank's obligation is defined by the terms of the LC alone, and the sale contract is irrelevant. The defenses available to the buyer arising out of the sale contract do not concern the bank and in no way affect its liability.

Types of letters of credit can be different. The most commonly used types of L/C are Irrevocable Letter of Credit, Confirmed Letter of Credit, and Sight Payment Credit.

- **Irrevocable Letter of Credit**

In this type of L/C, without the permissions from beneficiary or any parties related any change (amendment) or cancellation of the L/C (except it is expired) should be done by the Applicant through the issuing Bank. Whether to accept or reject the changes depends on the beneficiary.

- **Confirmed Letter of Credit**

An L/C is said to be confirmed when another bank adds its additional confirmation (or guarantee) to honor a complying presentation at the request or authorization of the issuing bank.

- **Sight Payment Credit**

It is a kind of credit. After observing the carriage documents from the seller and checking all the documents, the announcer bank immediately pays the required money. It is usually printed with "available by payment at sight".

 Useful Expression

结 算 用 语	
accept 承兑	D/P at sight 即期付款交单
advising/notifying bank 通知行	days of grace 宽限期
applicant/opener 开证申请人/开证人	debit advice 付讫借记通知
bank credit 银行信用	debtor 债权人
banker's draft 银行汇票	depreciate/appreciate 贬/升值
beneficiary 受益人	dishonour 拒付
bill of exchange; bill/draft 汇票	documentary collection 跟单托收
C. O. D. (Cash on delivery) 交货后付款	documentary draft 跟单汇票
C. W. O. (cash with order) 随订单付现	documentary L/C 跟单信用证
check 支票	draw a bill of exchange on 向……开汇票
collecting bank 代收行	drawee 受票人
collection 托收	drawer 出票人
commercial documents 商业单据	face value 票面价值
commercial draft 商业汇票	hard/soft currency 硬币/软币
confirming bank 保兑行	letter of credit 信用证
crossed check 划线支票	M/T(mail transfer)信汇
D/D (remittance by banker's demand draft)票汇	O/A trade: open account trade 赊账贸易
D/P after sight 远期付款交单	operative instruments 有效票据

续表

结 算 用 语	
payment against document 凭单付款	remittance fee 汇费
payment balance 货款尾数/余额	remittance 汇付
payment currency 支付货币	remitter 汇款人
payment in advance 预付货款	settlement of the payment 货款结算
payment order 支付通知书	sight/demand draft 即期汇票
present 提示	subsequent party 后手
prior party 前手	T/R(trust receipt) 信托收据
promissory note 本票	tenor 期限
recourse 追索	time/usance draft 远期汇票
remittance against documents 凭单付汇	type of remittance 汇款方式

Unit 12

Claim and Settlement

Learning Objectives

- To master the procedure of making a claim
- To know the methods of settling a claim
- To learn the key words and expressions in claim and settlement

Skill Developing Objectives

- To develop communication skills in claim and settlement
- To develop writing skills in claim and settlement

Section 1 Theme Lead-in

Read the following passage to get a better understanding of this unit.

Claim and Settlement

In the process of contract execution, the contracting parties should strictly fulfill their contractual obligations. If one party fails to fulfill the contract, it will bring trouble to the other, or sometimes the other party may suffer economic losses. Once this occurs, the injured party is entitled compensation under the contract or requires the responsible party to take remedial measures. The action the injured party taken is called "claims". The responsible party processing the request presented by the injured party is called "settlement".

Parties to be claimed include the seller, the buyer, shipping company and the insurance company. The types for claims are listed below:

Trade claim

Trade claim means that the trading parties claim for compensation on the contract basis, one party to another or both parties to opposite sides. It includes inferior, ineffective packing, breakage, shortage, or delayed shipment.

Transportation claim

Transportation claim means that the shipper or consignee can claim for the compensation to the transport contractor or his agent on the basis of contract. It includes non-delivery, short landed, missing, and change of sailing, rough handling and so on.

Insurance claim

Insurance claim means that the party who signs the contract with the insurer and enjoys insured interest claims for compensation to the insurer by the insurance policy when the goods encounter risk losses which are within the under writing scope.

The bases of claims include legal basis and factual basis and both are indispensable. Legal basis means sales contract and applicable law basis. Factual basis refers to the facts and details of the default and the written documents. It mainly includes several inspection certificates.

There are some issues to be paid attention to when making a claim. You must lay emphasis on the facts and find out the responsibility for the faults. Abide by the deadline for claim. Correctly ascertain the items and amount of the claim and prepare all the claim documents.

There are also some issues to be paid attention to related to the settlements of claim. Analyze whether the claim arguments from the opposite are adequate or not, whether the condition is true, whether the losses are caused by your side and whether the claims are according to the contract and the law. If the claims exceed the time limit, the party being claimed won't accept and attend to.

The content of claim is different. You can request compensation. You can request resupply for deficient or short delivery of goods. You can request exchange if the quality or specification of the goods do not match as stated. You can request repairs for machinery malfunction or damage. You can request reduction or depreciation for delivery delays or poor quality. You can also reject the goods, request refund of the goods and claim for the compensation.

 Notes

1. In the process of contract execution, the contracting parties should strictly fulfill their contractual obligations.
   在合同的执行过程中,签约双方应该严格履行合同义务。
2. Once this occurs, the injured party is entitled compensation under the contract or requires the responsible party to take remedial measures.
   这种情况一旦发生,受损方有权根据合同规定要求责任方赔偿或采取补救措施。
3. The action the injured party taken is called "claims". The responsible party processing the request presented by the injured party is called "settlements".
   受损方所采取的这种行动称之为"索赔";责任方就受损方提出的要求进行处理,叫做"理赔"。
4. Trade claim means that the trading parties claim for compensation on the contract basis, one party to another or both parties to opposite sides. It includes inferior, ineffective packing, breakage, shortage, or delayed shipment.
   贸易索赔是指贸易当事人以所订合同为基础,一方向另一方或双方向对方同时提出的索赔,包括品质不良、包装不良、破损、短装、延迟装运等。
5. Transportation claim means that the shipper or consignee can claim for the compensation to the transport contractor or his agent on the basis of contract. It includes non-delivery, short landed, missing, and change of sailing, rough handling and so on.
   运输索赔是指托运人或收货人依据所订合同向承运人或其代理人提出的索赔,包括未抵、短卸、遗失、更改航程、野蛮装卸等。

6. Insurance claim means that the party who signs the contract with the insurer and enjoys insured interest claims for compensation to the insurer by the insurance policy when the goods encounter risk losses which are within the under writing scope.
保险索赔是指和保险人签订保险合同并享有保险利益的一方，在货物遇到属于承保责任范围的风险损失时，凭保险单及有关证件向保险人提出的索赔。

7. Abide by the deadline for claim. Correctly ascertain the items and amount of the claim and prepare all the claim documents.
遵守索赔期限。准确确定索赔项目与金额并备齐索赔所需单证。

8. The bases of claims include legal basis and factual basis and both are indispensable.
索赔依据包括法律依据和事实依据，二者缺一不可。

9. Legal basis means sales contract and applicable law basis.
法律依据主要指买卖合同和适用的法律依据。

10. Factual basis refers to the facts and details of the default and the written documents. It mainly includes several inspection certificates.
事实依据是指违约的事实、情节及其书面证明。主要是各种检验证书。

11. Analyze whether the claim arguments from the opposite are adequate or not, whether the condition is true, whether the losses are caused by your side and whether the claims are according to the contract and the law.
认真研究分析对方索赔理由是否充足，情况是否属实，对方遭受的损失是否由你方造成，索赔是否符合合同及法律规定。

12. If the claims exceed the time limit, the party being claimed won't accept and attend to.
提出的索赔如属逾期，被索赔方可以不予受理。

13. You can request resupply for deficient or short delivery of goods.
货物短少或短交时，可请求补运。

14. You can request exchange if the quality or specification of the goods do not match as stated.
货物的品质不符或规格不符，可请求调换

15. You can request repairs for machinery malfunction or damage.
机器等发生故障或损坏时，可要求修理。

16. You can request reduction or depreciation for delivery delays or poor quality.

如交货延迟、品质不佳，皆可要求减价或贬值折让。
17. You can also reject the goods, request refund of the goods and claim for the compensation.
也可以拒收货物、请求退还货款，并赔偿损失。

 Problems Solving

1. What kinds of compensation are mentioned in the passage?
2. Whether the following statement is true or false according to the passage?
(1) The action the responsible party taken is called "claims".　　　( )
(2) The legal basis and factual basis of a claim can be dispensable.　　　( )
(3) There is no time limit to a claim.　　　( )
(4) You can request reduction or depreciation for delivery delays.　　　( )
(5) Transportation claim means that the shipper can claim for the compensation to the transport contractor or his agent on the basis of contract.　　　( )

 # Section 2　Conversations and Warm-up

 Conversations

Conversation 1　Serving Skill for Complaining Customers

(*A and B are the receptionists in different companies. They are talking with each other about the experiences in communicating with different customers.*)

A: Do you know how to deal with a complaining customer?

B: No matter by what way, don't get angry with them. It is better to communicate with a complaining customer, using the following steps to help you handle and solve the problem.

A: What's your suggestion?

B: Firstly, you should listen and take notes. Write down any names, dates, and major points of the complaint.

A: Well, I agree with you, and go on.

B: Secondly, think twice before making promises. Express your regret for his or her dissatisfaction and any inconvenience he or she may have experienced, but think before you give any promise—because nothing annoys customers more than a broken promise.

A: That's the exact question.

B: Thirdly, check the facts. Make sure the information the customer has given you is correct and work out solutions by yourself.

A: Yes. To respect the facts is the basis. What should I do next?

B: The last step is to offer solutions. When the customer complains, you should always offer him a solution to the problem. If you cannot directly fix the problem, offer him something else to try and keep him satisfied.

A: What does the customer service to do is to solve various problems?

B: There are many different types of solutions which could turn a disappointed customer into a happy one, such as, to offer a replacement, refund the money, offer a repair, offer a discount on the next purchase, and apologize for the inconvenience caused.

 Conversation 2   Accept a Claim

(*A is an exporter, who is speaking with B, Mr. Smith, the sales manager in a shipping company.*)

A: Hello, Mr. Smith. I'd like to talk about the damage of some goods that you delivered.

B: I am sorry to hear that.

A: Well, you see, you have probably been advised of the damage done to the foot wears. Upon its arrival in Africa on board S. S. Hope, it was found, much to our regret, that about 5% of the goods were broken.

B: Just a minute, Mr. Smith. Have your people in Capetown discovered what the exact causes of the damage were?

A: Yes. The damage of some foot wears occurring en route is due to careless handling and packaging in shipment and transportation.

B: Okay. In this case, we should hold the responsibility.

A: Thank you for your consideration. We wish our friendship and cooperation further develop in the future.

 Conversation 3   Refuse a Claim

(*A is Mr. Zhang, a receptionist of DHL Company, who is speaking with B, Mr. Smith from Jiangsu Food Company.*)

A: DHL Company. What can I do for you?

B: This is Jim Smith from Jiangsu Food Company. We regret to complain about the late delivery of canned mushroom under Contract No. AC42d.

A: I am sorry to hear that. Let me check for you. Oh, yes, the delivery will be made in the middle of September.

B: Yes. Although you guaranteed a delivery in the middle of September, we haven't received the goods till now. Your behavior is so disappointing that we cannot but lodge a claim against you.

A: I am sorry. But the delay is due to the bad weather.

B: We concluded the contract with you on the basis of your assurance.

A: Yes. You are right.

B: Unfortunately, late delivery has occurred several times recently, and we have no choice but to make it clear that business will be canceled in this case.

A: We apologize for the inconvenience.

B: We feel it necessary to clarify that if the supplier can not deliver the goods on time, we are unable to explain to our customers. We hope you can understand our situation and understand that we have to lodge a claim against you. We hope that you can offer more discount, at least extra 2%, to make compensation for the delay.

A: We apologize for the inconvenience. But the delay of the delivery was due to the bad weather, which was unexpected. According to the contract stipulations, we are not liable for the delay.

B: Okay. I see, you mean you refuse to take the responsibility for the delay?

A: Sorry. We regret to tell you that we cannot accept the requirement you proposed in your claim. We hope we will have good cooperation later and thank you for your understanding.

B: All right. If you can not settle this claim amicably through negotiation, we would have no choice but to submit it to the arbitration for settlement.

 Warm-up

A. Match the definitions in Column B with the terms in Column A.

A	B
1. submit	A. a restriction that is insisted upon as a condition for an agreement
2. stipulation	B. a resolution method for business disputes
3. complaint	C. hand over something formally
4. compensation	D. something given or received as payment or reparation
5. arbitration	E. a pleading describing some wrong or offense

B. The following is a passage about packaging. Fill in the blanks with the words given in the box and discuss with your partners about the importance of packaging.

| admit | manner | justified | treated | complaint |

In business activities, no matter how perfect an organization may be, complaints from the customers are certain to arise. There are some rules for dealing with a (1) _____. The first thing that has to be decided is whether the complaint is (2) _____. If so, then you have to (3) _____ it readily; express your regret and promise to put matters right. If the complaint is not justified, point this out politely and in an agreeable (4) _____. If you cannot deal with a complaint promptly, acknowledge it at once. Explain that you are looking into it and that you will send a full reply later. All complaints should be (5) _____ as serious matters and thoroughly investigated.

C. Make up a dialogue according to the following situation.

Student A works as a clerk in East Star Transportation Co., Ltd. and Student B is a client whose consignment has been damaged en route. Student A and Student B will act out the dialogue about claim and settlement.

The dialogue should cover the following information: greetings, the reason why to lodge a claim, and the settlement to the claim.

Section 3 Format Writings and Practical Usages

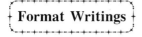

After reading the following passage, you are required to discuss with your partners and to complete the statements that follow the questions.

How to Make a Claim

Claim is the demand made by one party to another for a certain amount of compensation on account of a loss sustained through its negligence. There are several types of claim. They are claim regarding selling and buying, claim regarding transportation and claim concerning insurance.

You can make a claim either by phone or in letters. Generally, if you have to make a claim, there may be some emotions involved such as anger or frustration. The best claim makers are those that stick to the facts of the claim. Try to keep all emotion out of it.

When making a claim, plan your speech or letter as follows: First, begin by regretting the need to complain. Second, mention the date of the order, the date of delivery and the goods complained about. Then, state your reasons for being dissatisfied and ask for an explanation. Besides, refer to the inconvenience caused. Last but not least, suggest how the matter should be put right.

When lodging a claim, there are some documents required, such as Original Insurance Policy or Insurance Certificate, Contract of Affreightment, Commercial Invoice, Weight Memo, Packing List, Survey Report, Certificate of Loss or Damage and any correspondence with the carrier or any other party who could be responsible for the loss or damage.

Problems Solving

1. What types of claim are mentioned in the passage?
2. In what ways can you make a claim?
3. What kind of emotions do you generally have when making a claim?
4. According to the passage, what steps should you take when making a claim?
5. What documents should you prepare when you lodge a claim?

Writing Samples

Letter 1　Making a Claim

May 15, 2024

Dear Sir,

　　Re: Claim on Bread-making Machines

The captioned goods you shipped per S. S. "Happy Valley" on May 14 arrived here yesterday.

On examination, we have found that many of the bread-making machines are severely damaged, though the cases themselves show no trace of damage.

Considering this damage was due to the rough handling by the steamship company, we are therefore, compelled to claim on you to compensate us for the loss, $27,500, which we have sustained by the damage to the goods.

We trust that you will be kind enough to accept this claim and deduct the sum claimed from the amount of your next invoice to us.

Sincerely,

Letter 2   Settlement to a Claim

May 24, 2024

Dear Sirs,

Re: Contract No. FX-261-Bread-Making Machines

We thank you for your letter of May 15, with enclosures, claiming for damage on the consignment of the bread-making machines shipped per S/S "Happy Valley".

On examination we found that the bread-making machines had not been fixed tightly in the case, which caused many of bread-making machines damaged en route. As you know the consignment was delivered by FCL and as stipulated in the contract, when the cases show no trace of damage outside, we shall not be liable for the damage of the consignment.

But in view of our long-standing business relations, we can offer you an extra 10% discount.

We look forward to your early reply.

Yours faithfully,

Letter 3   Settlement to a Claim

May 25, 2024

Dear Sirs,

Re: Settlement to a Claim on Woolen Goods

We are in receipt of your letter of May 24 and regret to note your complaint respecting the Woolen Goods we sent you by S.S. "Union".

We have looked up the matter in our records, and so far as we can find, the goods in question were in first class condition when they left here, as was evidenced by the Bill of Lading. It is therefore quite obvious that the damage complained of must have taken place in transit. In the circumstances, we are apparently not liable for the damage and would advise you to claim on the shipping company who should be held responsible.

At any rate, we thank you for bringing this to our attention and we shall be pleased to take the matter up on your behalf with the shipping company concerned.

Yours faithfully,

Practical Usages

1. Making a Claim 提出索赔

1) State the reasons why claims are made
   声明索赔的原因

- On examination, we have found that many of the bread-making machines are severely damaged, though the cases themselves show no trace of damage.
  经检查,我们发现许多面包机严重损坏,尽管包装箱表面没有破损。

- Your shipment of our Order No. 630 has been found short weight by 220 kilos.
  现发现你方所发运的我方 630 号订单货物短重 220 公斤。

2) Propose the specific claim
   提出具体索赔要求

- Considering this damage was due to the rough handling by the steamship company, we are therefore, compelled to claim on you to compensate us for the loss, $27,500.
  考虑到破损是因为运输公司野蛮装卸造成的,我们不得不提出索赔,索赔金额 27500 美元。

- We ask for replacement by the correct number in the nearest future.
  我们要求尽快运来数量无误的替换货物。

2. Settlement to a Claim 理赔

1) State the result of investigation
   声明调查结果

- On examination we found that the bread-making machines had not been fixed tightly within the case, which caused many of bread-making machines damaged en route.
  经调查我们发现,面包机在箱内没有固定,导致大量面包机运输途中受损。

- We have looked up the matter in our records, and so far as we can find, the goods in question were in first class condition when they left here, as was evidenced by the Bill of Lading.
  我们查看了记录,就目前来看,货物发运时完好,提单可以证明这一点。

2) Offer settlement to the claim
   提出解决方案

- But in view of our long-standing business relations, we can offer you an extra 10% discount.

考虑到我们的长期合作关系，我们愿意给予你方额外 10% 的折扣。

- We shall be pleased to take the matter up on your behalf with the shipping company concerned.

我们很荣幸代表贵方与运输公司协商解决此事。

Problems Solving

1. The following is a letter of complaints. Fill in the blanks with the words given below.

| unreliable | delays | normally | dealing | demand |

Dear Mr. Smith,

We have been (1) _____ with your company for three years. During that time, we have been more than satisfied with your freight services. Our goods are (2) _____ dealt with promptly, which gives us ample time to meet the (3) _____ for our goods.

However, recently you have started to deliver later than agreed, and your service is becoming very (4) _____. On two occasions, we have failed to meet our own deadlines due to your (5) _____.

We should like you to deliver our goods timely and keep our cooperation further.

Yours sincerely,

2. Suppose you have received the above Letter 1. Write a letter to reply, stating the result of your investigation and the proposal for the settlement to the claim.

Section 4　Skills Training and Case Study Samples

Skills Training

A. There are ten incomplete sentences in this part. For each sentence there are three choices marked A, B and C. Choose the one that best completes the sentence.

1. All complaints should be treated as serious matters and thoroughly _____.
   A. investigated　　B. settled　　C. mentioned

2. Claim is the demand for a certain amount of _____.
   A. comprise　　B. compensation　　C. constitute

3. The damage of the consignment was _____ the rough handling by the shipping company.

A. because   B. due to   C. since

4. We shall not be _____ for the damage of the consignment.

A. liable   B. capable   C. reliable

5. We shall be pleased to take the matter up on your _____ with the shipping company concerned.

A. stuff   B. situation   C. behalf

6. When handling claims and complaints, you must judge whether the complaints and claims are _____.

A. justified   B. good   C. fault

7. When the loss is not serious, the party suffered the loss may not _____ a claim for compensation.

A. accept   B. suppose   C. lodge

8. If the claims exceed the time limit, our side won't accept and _____ to.

A. extend   B. achieve   C. attend

9. You can request resupply for _____ or short delivery of goods.

A. sufficient   B. deficient   C. efficient

10. You can request _____ for delivery delays or poor quality

A. reduction   B. conduction   C. induction

B. Translate the following terms into English.

向某人提出索赔   理赔
抱怨   损失
短卸   减价
赔偿   退还
拒收   违约

C. Translate the following sentences into Chinese.

1. You assured us that you could deliver the curtains within one week, yet this has not happened.
2. Unfortunately, you have sent us the wrong items.
3. We are not happy about the inconvenience that the situation is causing us.
4. We should be obliged if you would replace the goods you delivered with the correct ones.
5. If you do not refund all of the money we have paid, we shall have no choice but to seek legal advice in the matter.

{ Case Study Samples }

Sample 1

Arbitration

Arbitration, a form of alternative dispute resolution (ADR), is a technique for the resolution of disputes outside the courts, where the parties to a dispute refer it to one or more persons (the "arbitrators", "arbiters" or "arbitral tribunal"), by whose decision (the "award") they agree to be bound. It is a resolution technique in which a third party reviews the evidence in the case and imposes a decision that is legally binding for both sides and enforceable. Other forms of ADR include mediation (a form of settlement negotiation facilitated by a neutral third party) and non-binding resolution by experts. Arbitration is often used for the resolution of commercial disputes, particularly in the context of international commercial transactions. The use of arbitration is also frequently employed in consumer and employment matters, where arbitration may be mandated by the terms of employment or commercial contracts.

Arbitration can be either voluntary or mandatory (although mandatory arbitration can only come from a statute or from a contract that is voluntarily entered into, where the parties agree to hold all existing or future disputes to arbitration, without necessarily knowing, specifically, what disputes will ever occur) and can be either binding or non-binding. Non-binding arbitration is similar to mediation in that a decision cannot be imposed on the parties. However, the principal distinction is that whereas a mediator will try to help the parties find a middle ground on which to compromise, the (non-binding) arbitrator remains totally removed from the settlement process and will only give a determination of liability and, if appropriate, an indication of the quantum of damages payable. By one definition arbitration is binding and so non-binding arbitration is technically not arbitration.

Arbitration is a proceeding in which a dispute is resolved by an impartial adjudicator whose decision the parties to the dispute have agreed, or legislation has decreed, will be final and binding. There are limited rights of review and appeal of arbitration awards.

Problems Solving

1. What is arbitration?

2. What is binding or non-binding arbitration?
3. Negotiation, arbitration, and litigation are the three primary ways to resolve commercial disputes. Could you tell the advantage and disadvantage of each way?

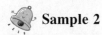 **Sample 2**

How to File a Freight Claim for Loss, Damage or Delay

The first point to know is that a claim against a carrier is a legal demand for the payment of money arising from the breach of the contract of carriage (usually the bill of lading).

Claims rules will be found either in carriers' tariffs or in their bills of lading, or both. Court decisions interpret these regulations, laws and tariffs, and determine the rights and obligations of the parties.

What constitutes a claim?

No specific claim form is prescribed by law, but four elements are essential: (1) The shipment must be identified to enable the carrier to conduct an investigation; (2) The type of loss or damage must be stated; (3) The amount of the claim must be stated or estimated; and (4) A demand for payment by the carrier must be made.

The shipment identification information must include the carrier's "Pro number", shipper's number, vehicle number, origin date, delivery date, and commodity description.

The claimant's name must be either (1) the entity having title to the goods in transit; (2) the entity assuming the risk of loss in transit; or (3) an assignee of either (1) or (2).

The carrier against whom the claim may be filed is either the originating carrier or the delivering carrier.

It is not recommended that claims be filed against intermediate connecting carriers, although it is permissible to do so if it is definitely known which carrier caused the loss or damage.

The claim must be delivered to the carrier within the time period specified in the carrier's contract and/or tariff, or that time prescribed by law (usually nine months from the delivery). Since the date of receipt by the carrier determines whether or not the claim is timely filed, claims should be filed via delivery methods which give some type of confirmation of receipt and guarantee as to length of time for delivery, such as Facsimile transmission (FAX); Registered or Certified mail, Return Receipt Requested (RRR); Express Mail; Express Courier Services; Electronic Data Interchange (EDI).

Supporting documentation

Claims must usually be supported by

a. The original bill of lading;
b. The paid freight bill;
c. Proof of the value of the commodities lost or damaged;
d. Inspection reports, if made;
e. Copies of request for inspection;
f. Notification of loss;
g. Waiver of inspection by carrier;
h. Special documents when appropriate, such as photographs.

Suit deadlines

If a carrier denies liability for a loss for which the claimant has reason to believe the carrier is lawfully liable, the claimant has the right to institute a lawsuit. However, such suits must be instituted within strict time limits. The most commonly applicable suit time limit is two years and one day from the date the carrier disallowed the claim.

 Problems Solving

1. What constitutes a claim? Make a three-minute presentation to make an introduction. You can use some visual aid to help you to express yourself, such as a flowchart, a diagram or a PPT.
2. Is there any time limit for a claimant to lodge a claim? Surf the internet to the time limit for a claim in different countries.

 Section 5 Elevating Vision and Useful Expressions

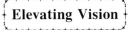

Force Majeure

Force majeure is a common clause in contracts that essentially frees both parties from liability or obligation when an extraordinary event or circumstance beyond the control of the parties or an event described by the legal term Acts of God, prevents one or both parties from fulfilling their obligations under the contract. In practice, most force majeure clauses do not excuse a party's non-performance entirely, but only suspends it for the duration of the force majeure.

Force majeure is generally intended to include risks beyond the reasonable control of a party, incurred not as a product or result of the negligence or malfeasance of a party, which have a materially adverse effect on the ability of such party to perform its obligations, as where non-performance is caused by the usual and natural consequences of external forces (for example, predicted rain stops an outdoor event), or where the intervening circumstances are specifically contemplated.

A party is not liable for a failure to perform any of its obligations if he proves that the failure was due to an impediment beyond his control and that he could not reasonably be expected to have taken the impediment into account at the time of the conclusion of the contract or to have avoided or overcome it or its consequences.

The following is an example of how force majeure might be described in a specific contract.

Clause 19 Force Majeure

A party is not liable for failure to perform the party's obligations if such failure is as a result of Acts of God (including fire, flood, earthquake, storm, hurricane or other natural disaster), war, invasion, act of foreign enemies, hostilities (regardless of whether war is declared), civil war, rebellion, revolution, insurrection, military or usurped power or confiscation, terrorist activities, nationalization, government sanction, blockage, embargo, labor dispute, strike, lockout or interruption or failure of electricity or telephone service. No party is entitled to terminate this Agreement under Clause 17 (Termination) in such circumstances.

If a party asserts Force Majeure as an excuse for failure to perform the party's obligation, then the nonperforming party must prove that the party took reasonable steps to minimize delay or damages caused by foreseeable events, that the party substantially fulfilled all non-excused obligations, and that the other party was timely notified of the likelihood or actual occurrence of an event described in Clause 19 (Force Majeure).

After signing the contract, if an accident which is not because of the fault or negligence of the parties but because of something which cannot be predicted, prevented, conquered or avoided makes the contract cannot be fulfilled timely, the party suffered the accident can exempt or delay the execution of the contract.

Useful Expression

索 赔 用 语	
arbitral award 仲裁裁决	package breakage 包装破损
Certificate of Insurance 保险单	quality discrepancy 品质规格与合同不符
claim against carrier 向承运人索赔	reject a claim 拒绝索赔
claimant 索赔人	relinquish a claim 撤回索赔
claims settling fee 理赔代理费	settle a claim 解决索赔
claims surveying agent 理赔检验代理人	short delivery 短交
Weight Note 磅码单	short unloaded 短卸
Damage Report 破损证明	Shortage Landing Report Certificate 短卸证明
entertain a claim 受理索赔	signed claims settling agent 理赔代理人
Evaluation Sheet 修理费及其估价书	Survey Report 公证报告
inferior quality 品质不良	Surveyor's Report 鉴定报告
Inspection Certificate 检验证书	waive a claim 放弃索赔
lost in transit 短失	Weight Certificate 重量证明书
Marine Protest 海难	withdraw a claim 撤回索赔

References

1. 王传见.国际货代物流实务英语手册.武汉:华东理工大学出版社,2004.
2. 姚大伟.国际贸易单证实务.北京:中国对外贸易出版社,2005.
3. 王斌义.国际物流人员业务操作指引.北京:对外经济贸易大学出版社,2005.
4. 中国国际货运代理协会.国际货运代理专业英语.北京:中国商务出版社,2009.
5. 中国国际货运代理协会.国际货物运输代理概论.北京:中国商务出版社,2010.
6. 张洁楠,莫天宇.报关英语.广州:华南理工大学出版社,2010.
7. 中国国际货运代理协会.国际海上货运代理理论与实务.北京:中国商务出版社,2010.
8. 中国国际货运代理协会.国际航空货运代理理论与实务.北京:中国商务出版社,2010.
9. 中国国际货运代理协会.国际陆路货运代理与多式联运理论与实务.北京:中国商务出版社,2010.
10. 王传见.国际货代物流实务英语手册(第2版).上海:华东理工大学出版社,2011.
11. 陈鑫.报关与国际货运专业英语(第4版).天津:天津大学出版社,2012.
12. 陆佳平.包装标准化和质量法规.北京:印刷工业出版社,2013.
13. 明国英.货运代理师专业英语.北京:中国人民大学出版社,2013.
14. 王之泰.中国物流业创新的一些思考.中国流通经济,2013(4):8-12.
22. 全国人民代表大会.中华人民共和国进出口商品检验法.北京:法律出版社,2013.
23. 王海文.新编物流设施设备.北京:清华大学出版社,2014.
24. 荣瑾.中国海关报关与国际货运专业英语.北京:中国海关出版社,2014.
25. 董娜.国际货运代理专业英语辅导与全真试题.南京:南京大学出版社,2014.
26. 彭影.现代物流综合实训教程.成都:西南交通大学出版社,2014.
27. 国家质检总局法规司,国家质检总局标准法规中心译.中华人民共和国进出口商品检验法实施条例.北京:中国标准出版社,2015.
28. 黄伟军.国际集装箱海上运输与货运代理.北京:中国人民大学出版社,2015.
29. 张为群.国际货运代理实务操作(第3版).成都:西南财经大学出版社,2015.
30. 中国国际货运代理协会.新编国际货运代理专业英语.北京:中国商务出版社,2015.
31. 王国石.报关与国际货运专业英语.大连:东北财经大学出版社,2015.
32. 周宁.物流英语(第3版).北京:电子工业出版社,2015.
33. 楼前飞.国际货代专业英语语料库.杭州:浙江工商大学出版社,2015.
34. 陈春慧.货运代理英语实务.北京:中国商务出版社,2016.
35. 胡惟璇.国际货运实用英语.北京:化学工业出版社,2016.
36. 牛薇妮.国际货代英语.北京:中国人民大学出版社,2016.
37. 仲颖.物流专业英语(第2版).北京:北京大学出版社,2017.
38. 朱岩.国际货运代理实务业务训练.杭州:浙江工商大学出版社,2017.
39. 周晓晔.物流专业英语(第2版).北京:机械工业出版社,2018.
40. 吴金卓.物流英语.北京:中国财富出版社,2020.

教师服务

感谢您选用清华大学出版社的教材！为了更好地服务教学，我们为授课教师提供本书的教学辅助资源，以及本学科重点教材信息。请您扫码获取。

▶▶ 教辅获取

本书教辅资源，授课教师扫码获取

▶▶ 样书赠送

物流与供应链管理类重点教材，教师扫码获取样书

 清华大学出版社

E-mail: tupfuwu@163.com
电话：010-83470332 / 83470142
地址：北京市海淀区双清路学研大厦 B 座 509
网址：https://www.tup.com.cn/
传真：8610-83470107
邮编：100084